D0812322

LATIN AMERICAN HISTORICAL DICTIONARIES SERIES
Edited by A. Curtis Wilgus

*Latin American Historical Dictionaries,
No. 20*

Historical Dictionary

of

PERU

by

Marvin Alisky

The Scarecrow Press, Inc.
Metuchen, N.J., & London 1979

Library of Congress Cataloging in Publication Data

Álisky, Marvin.
  Historical dictionary of Peru.

  (Latin American Historical dictionaries ; no. 20)
  Bibliography: p.
  1. Peru--History--Dictionaries. I. Title.
F3404.A39   985'.003   79-16488
ISBN 0-8108-1235-5

CONTENTS

EDITOR'S FOREWORD

Peru was the last stronghold of the Spaniards in South America. The transition to independence, guided and stimulated by Simón Bolívar and José de Sucre, brought an end to colonization. But the path of the new government, with Bolivia (Upper Peru) separated as an independent state, was not smooth. For more than a century following, the country had its share of political factions and parties and political documents and constitutions. Personalism has dominated its national life during several generations, and internal and external friction has affected its political, economic, social and cultural development. Dr. Álisky has caught the spirit of the country and its people, and he has selected items for inclusion in his book which aim to present a logical and balanced dictionary rather than an encyclopedia.

Since 1960 the author has been a professor of Political Science at Arizona State University. In 1965 he was the founder and first Director of the Center for Latin American Studies at that institution. In various related academic and professional capacities he has been associated with Indiana University, Trinity University, University of California, Irvine, Princeton University, National University of Nicaragua, Catholic University at Lima, University of Cuzco and University of Arequipa.

Over the years, one of Dr. Álisky's interests has been mass communication. He has been associated with NBC in Arizona, in the Southwest, in Latin America and in Spain. Along with these activities he has served as columnist for the Arizona Republic, the Tempe Daily News, the Indianapolis News and the Christian Science Monitor. In 1957 he was Scholarship chairman of the Inter-American Press Association. Civil affairs have also attracted his attention and he has held positions in city, state and national organizations, including the United States Department of State.

These wide interests and activities have resulted in

his preparing many publications which have appeared in the United States and Latin America. Since 1947 he has published more than 200 magazine, encyclopedia and yearbook articles and many newspaper columns. He has been author or co-author of ten books and monographs. A large proportion of his writings deal with Latin America, and many concern Peru directly or indirectly.

It is only natural that Dr. Álisky's publications should attract wide attention. As a result he has been honored by institutions in the United States, Mexico, Ecuador, Uruguay and Peru. He belongs to a number of professional academic groups in the United States and elsewhere and he has served them in various capacities, including that of advisor to Sophia University in Tokyo. Moreover, in 1960 he was a delegate to the UNESCO conference, Quito, Ecuador; in 1965 he was an Associate Scholar at the inter-parliamentary Conference, La Paz, Baja California, Mexico; and in 1973 he served as Research Associate at the Colegio de Mexico. For five years (1957-1962) he was a guest lecturer at the American Institute of Foreign Trade. Since 1960 he has been an Honorary Citizen of Ecuador.

I am happy that Dr. Álisky is now a contributor to this Historical Dictionary Series.

A. Curtis Wilgus,
Emeritus Director,
School of Inter American
Studies,
University of Florida

INTRODUCTION

I

This book compiles historical, geographical, political, economic, and cultural facts and figures, blended so as to provide a source of information on the public life of Peru.

Geographical entries include the twenty-four Departments into which this unitary republic is divided for administrative purposes, with cross-references to major provinces, the subdivisions within each department. Major cities also are listed and described.

National leaders sketched herein range from pre-Conquest Incas to generals in the struggle for independence from Spain, to 19th-century caudillos or strong-man presidents, to 20th-century reformers, both military and civilian.

Political parties covered range from the large and significant Aprista movement of Víctor Raúl Haya de la Torre to the smaller personalistic groups behind such military leaders as the late General Manuel Odría.

Wherever possible, statistics are current as of early 1978. Sources for data range from Peruvian government annual reports, Organization of American States documents, and periodical literature, to key interviews with top leaders of Peru conducted by the author during June, July, and August of 1977 in Lima, Arequipa, and Cuzco. I also received valuable information from specialists on Peru in the Department of State and from colleagues in academia.

Any thank-you list runs the risk of leaving out some individuals who were helpful. But I must single out for special thanks David Scott Palmer, chairman of the Latin America Area Studies Program of the Foreign Service Institute in Washington, D. C. , though this in no way implies that the State Department endorses my own estimations of the political

1

nature of any of the Peruvians discussed.   All such evalua-
tions are strictly my own.

As a political scientist, I needed to refocus my usual
emphasis on Peru from the present to the past.   I turned to
the writings of the historian from the University of Notre
Dame, Frederick B. Pike.   Especially helpful in launching
my research were Pike's Modern History of Peru (New York:
Praeger, 1967), and his The United States and the Andean
Republics (Cambridge: Harvard University Press, 1977).

David P. Werlich helped by sending me some advance
excerpts from his Peru: a Short History (Carbondale: Southern Illinois University Press, 1978).

Back in 1971, when I spent time in Peru writing my
monograph Peruvian Political Perspective (Tempe: Arizona
State University Center for Latin American Studies, 1972;
2nd edition, 1975), Luigi R. Einaudi, then with the Rand
Corporation, gave me invaluable advice.   He is now with the
Department of State and the notes I took in extended conver-
sations with him are now seven years old, yet they served
me again in 1977 and 1978, when compiling this dictionary.

Abraham F. Lowenthal, who edited The Peruvian Experiment (Princeton, N. J.:   Princeton University, 1975),
when in Lima in 1971, though very busy as director of the
Ford Foundation in Peru, generously made time for all my
questions as they arose, helping me reorient into Peruvian
life.   I had to recapture the attunement to Peru which I had
enjoyed in 1958, when I lectured at Catholic University in
Lima under Fulbright auspices.   The intervening years had
eroded a bit of that informal understanding of Peruvian life
and only new field work could recoup it.

Thanks to Professor Mark O. Dickerson of the University of Calgary for providing me with a Canadian perspective on Peru's attempt at social revolution.

Over the past twenty years, each stay in Lima has
always been made pleasant at my home away from home, the
Residencial Miramar of Mrs. Dolly Tupholme in Miraflores.

Back in the 1940s, when I was an undergraduate student and first discovered Latin America, one of the first au-
thors I read was A. Curtis Wilgus.   The Outline-History of
Latin America by Wilgus and Raul D'Eça (New York: Barnes

& Noble, 1943, 3rd edition) remained with me throughout wartime service in the navy, during a tour of duty as news correspondent for the National Broadcasting Company in Latin
America, and during my doctoral studies at the University of
Texas (1950-53), and now, a quarter-century after receiving
the Ph. D., that worn paperback with the faded green cover
still occupies a place of honor on my desk as a ready reference.   Beside it rests the blue covered paperback by Wilgus,
Readings in Latin American Civilization (New York: Barnes
& Noble, 1946).   Though hundreds and hundreds of other books
on Latin America have engulfed my mind since discovering
those two slim but fact-filled volumes, they remain a remind-
er to me of the happy days when I first became entwined
with Latin America professionally and personally.

Perhaps a few young students will stumble into an in-
tense interest in Peru by a chance encounter with this dictionary, and then will involve themselves more and more
with Latin America by reading the other dictionaries in this
Scarecrow Press series on Latin American nations.   If so,
some day they will tip their battered sombreros in a salute
also to Professor Wilgus and his Inter-American Bibliograph-
ical and Library Association.

II

Peru, old and new, displays its age in its setting and
people.   Stone masonry, old when the Spaniards arrived in
1532, still stands sturdily as sentinels of the past and links
to the present.   Indians in tiny Andean villages, in everyday
behavior, suggest a continuum of conduct that the Inca ruler
Atahualpa, the conqueror Pizarro, and the generals through
the 19th century must each in turn have witnessed.   Balsa
wood boats bobbing on the icy waters of Lake Titicaca, on
the surface of the world's highest navigable lake for steam-
ships, present an exotic picture which takes away the breath
of a first-time tourist as much as does the extremely high
altitude at the roof of the earth.

Haunting tunes played on wooden flutes by Quechuas
and Aymarás charm not only the herds of llamas, which are
the chief object of the players, but also any visitor within
earshot.

In metropolitan Lima, more than three million residents crowd the streets in a vehicular ballet saluting the

smoggy symbol of modernization, the traffic jam. High-rise
buildings with glass sides glisten beside the ornate colonial
structures bearing the imprint of Spain.

In provincial cities, marketing entities nurtured by the
basic industries of fishing, mining, farming, and ranching
hold forth in modern offices fronting century-old buildings,
with the business facade of the 1970s grafted onto a Peruvian
way of doing business formulated before adding machines, let
alone computerized bank statements.

In the small towns and villages where peasants--larg-
est segment of the Peruvian population--live, whistling winds
from the Andes speak the sounds of provincial life, whereas
gray clouds portray the sights of the coastal plain. High in
the sierra, Andean towns bathe in bright sunlight, while far
into the eastern slopes, jungles spread uninterrupted vegetation like a green blanket draped by nature.

On terraces and rugged hilly slopes, brown men open
the orange earth with wooden plows to plant corn and beans,
the sustenance of a similar civilization on the same sites
one thousand years before.

Potential progress from fledgling industries hum with
fishmeal processing on the coast, and modest outpourings of
consumer goods. Yet 1978 found the government forced into
austerity, cutting back social reform programs, painfully re-
ducing deficit-spending budgets, without achieving stability
for the sol, Peru's unit of currency.

As when the Spaniards overwhelmed the colorful Inca
Empire in the 1530s, so also in the 1970s new leaders strive
to remake old Peru into a new nation. And its resources
are abrim with promise: fish products, copper, oil, tim-
ber, iron, and silver. The goals of the 1980s, however, remain punctuated with the question-mark decisions of a new
generation of leaders not yet seasoned by experience.

Like ancient Gaul, all of Peru is divided into three
parts. The narrow seacoast has a 1,400-mile shoreline
facing the Pacific Ocean, and varies in width from eight to
seventy-five miles. This coastal plain comprises only 12
per cent of the area of the republic but contains more than
40 per cent of its total population. Despite an arid climate,
this costa sprouts agricultural oases in irrigated valleys, the
water coming from fifty-two rivers which empty into the

Pacific.   Within this coastal plain lies much of the industrial
activity of Peru.

Rising 10, 000 feet above sea level, the Andean mountain range demarcates the costa from the sierra or highlands
region.   The sierra, with 31 per cent of the total Peruvian
land area, has 55 per cent of the republic's population.
Since pre-Hispanic days, a majority of the Indians have remained in the Andes, to eke out a living in mining and agriculture.   In recent decades, they have been lured to the
coastal towns into the fishing and construction industries.

East of the sierra, the tropical forest and jungle or
selva accounts for 57 per cent of the national territory but
contains merely five per cent of Peru's estimated 1978 population of 16 million.

Despite a vast national territory equal to the combined
areas of the United Kingdom, Spain, and France, and a population seemingly small compared to those of Brazil, Mexico,
Argentina, and Colombia, the fact remains that in terms of
potable water, potential jobs, and roads and other land connections between cities, Peru demographically has become
crowded.

III

Culturally, Peru remains as old as the viceregal society which guided the hybrid cholo (Spanish-Indian) peasants.
Politically and economically, Peru reflects the reform attempts of ousted civilian President Fernando Belaúnde (1963-
1968), and the full-scale program of reforms of the military
government which came to power on October 3, 1968.   From
that date to August 29, 1975, the military reformers were
led by General Juan Velasco, who was replaced as President
of the Republic by General Francisco Morales Bermúdez.

In November 1962, Hugo Blanco, Marxist guerrilla
leader, attacked a police station near Cuzco and killed three
officers.   In May 1963, Blanco was captured, tried, and con-
victed, then sentenced to twenty-five years in prison.   Later
he was given the choice of remaining in prison or going into
exile.   Blanco got on an airplane for Sweden but often turned
up in Mexico at leftist rallies, and in 1977 toured the United
States, sponsored by various Mexican-American groups.   On
April 12, 1978, the government of President Morales permitted

him to return from exile. He was greeted at the Lima airport by thousands of workers of Marxist unions and student
federations organized by the Frente Obrero, Campesino,
Estudantil, y Popular or FOCEP (Popular Student, Farmer,
and Worker Federation). So much for the repeated charges
during 1977 and 1978 by various Peruvian and foreign Marxist groups and fronts that the Peruvian government under
General Morales was inhibiting the far-left from engaging in
political activities. Just the opposite has been true. The
Partido Socialista Revolucionario or PSR (Revolutionary Socialist Party) of General Leonidas Rodríguez Figueroa, who
was deposed as head of the government's SINAMOS agency
in 1976, received space in 1978 in newspapers and radio air
time in the campaign for the one hundred seats of the constituent assembly scheduled to be elected on June 18, 1978.
Rodríguez was deported after the election.

From late 1968 to late 1977, formal political party
activities and the Congress were suspended, as military
government ruled Peru.

On November 16, 1977, the next transition in the political system formulating the policies under which Peruvians
live was promulgated. June 18, 1978 was set as election day
for a constituent assembly, and 1980 was targeted for the
general elections which will return the government to civilian
hands.

During the past decade, Peruvian leaders have striven
to break the age-old strictures which have inhibited an up-
wardly mobile society. Reform laws dealing with petroleum,
other mining, agriculture, fishing, industries, and education
have spawned discernibly new procedures in both public and
private executive suites. The Center for Higher Military
Studies (CAEM) has nurtured a new breed of military leaders
dedicated to modernization and reforms. The Council of
Presidential Advisors (COAP) has helped Presidents Velasco
and Morales Bermúdez formulate policies to carry out elaborate reform programs.

As this book goes to press, Peru perches on still another rung of the never-ending ladder of public administration, which serves as the vantage point from which to analyze
Peruvian history, past and in the making. Factors have been
set in motion to curtail a dynamic period of military government and try another era of civilian rule.

Certainly this republic, almost the size of Alaska or twice the size of Texas, with a population of more than sixteen million, deserves the attention of those seriously interested in Latin America. And for those merely beguiled by the innate exotic qualities of Peru, an up-to-date dictionary also will be helpful.

Marvin Álisky,
Arizona State University
Tempe, Arizona.
May 1978

THE DICTIONARY

ABASCAL, JOSE DE. Viceroy of Peru during 1806-1816. He governed Peru during a period when Spain's authority and political control of its vast American colonial empire began to be seriously challenged for the first time. When Abascal became Viceroy in 1806, Lima symbolized the bulwark of Spanish colonial power in Latin America as it had for nearly three centuries. Its bureaucracy was enormous and so committed to loyalty to the Spanish crown that Lima was called "little Madrid" throughout the Americas. In 1809, Abascal suppressed a revolution against Spanish authority sparked by rebels from Chile and Ecuador. The liberal Constitution of 1812 in Spain temporarily silenced the royalist cause in Peru. From 1812 to 1816, Peruvian patriots gained new members to their cause of political independence. Abascal's successor as Viceroy, Joaquín de Pezuela, inherited the staggering challenge of fighting General José de San Martín's army of liberation, which landed in Pisco and fought its way northward to Lima.

ABSENTEE LANDLORDS. The traditional agricultural production methods of absentee landlords owning huge estates was a target of reformers in the civilian administration of President Fernando Belaúnde during 1963-1968, and the military administration of President Juan Velasco during 1968-1975. By the time General Francisco Morales Bermúdez replaced General Velasco as president on August 29, 1975, sufficient expropriations and reforms had taken place so that resident owners and managers had replaced many traditional absentee landlords, both Peruvian aristocratic families and foreign corporations. Absentee owners for decades had been more concerned with taking their profits than with reinvesting in modern machinery and chemicals which could increase crop yields. During the 1960s, Peru's population was increasing 3.1 per cent a year, yet the

9

1969 agricultural output remained barely equal to that
of 1962. Potatoes are native to Peru, yet potato yields
in 1967 averaged 6,700 kilos per hectare (15,000 pounds
per 2.47 acres), whereas the world average was 12,700
kilos per hectare. Such data were cited in 1968 and
1969 as the military government promulgated expropriations against absentee landlords. Even the advent of
agricultural workers' communities or cooperatives, however, by 1977 had increased agricultural production only
modestly, from 14 to 16 per cent of Peru's Gross Do-
mestic Product.

ACCION POPULAR. The political party established in 1956
by Fernando Belaúnde. See BELAUNDE and POPULAR
ACTION.

AEROPERU. The national airline of Peru, established as a
government corporation in 1973 to fill the gap of the
defunct Aerolinas Peruanas, a privately-owned airline
which had gone bankrupt. Aeroperú, in turn, continued
to lose money on all international flights, and was reorganized on October 1, 1977, as a corporation with
both private and public stockholders. During 1978 sub-
stantial blocs of stock were scheduled to be sold to private Peruvian investment concerns. The government,
on August 1, 1977, recapitalized Aeroperú's U.S. $25
million debts. In return Aeroperú management pledged
to strive for an operations profit.

ALEGRIA, CIRO. Born in 1909 in Cajabamba, Peru, of
Spanish-Irish parents. Died in 1967. His great-grand-
father was an Irishman, Diego Lynch, owner of Peruvian mines. Alegría at age eighteen began work as a
newspaper reporter, covering politics and government.
Active in the American Popular Revolutionary Alliance
(Alianza Popular Revolucionaria Americana; APRA), he
became a political prisoner when APRA was outlawed
in 1931. In 1933 he was released into exile in Chile,
where he lived until his return to Peru in the 1950s.
He became Peru's leading novelist with the publication
of The Golden Serpent (La serpiente de oro) in 1935
and The Hungry Dogs (Los perros hambrientos) in 1939,
both of which won Chile's best novel award. Perros
is considered among the great novels of Spanish-language literature for its authentic portrayal of Peruvian
folklore and the insight with which the author portrays
his characters. In 1941 he published El mundo es

ancho y ajeno (Broad and Alien Is the World), which
won first prize for the best Latin American novel in the
contest of the Pan American Union.   This novel offers
a cryptic summary of Peruvian political life, with the
average Peruvian feeling that his "world orbit" is more
alien than wide.

ALIANZA POPULAR REVOLUCIONARIA AMERICANA.   The
American Popular Revolutionary Alliance (APRA) became Peru's first modern political party with a nationwide organization institutionalized to survive a succes-
sion of leaders, as contrasted with other Peruvian political parties, which until the middle of the 20th Century were personalistic groups not long surviving their
founders.   A young political reformer, Víctor Raúl
Haya de la Torre, was forced into exile in 1923 by
Peruvian dictator Augusto B. Leguía.   In Mexico City
in 1924, Haya created the APRA, conceived as a political movement to redress centuries of inequities suffered by millions of Indians and mestizos (Spanish-
Indian hybrids) at the hands of Spanish and other Euro-
pean-origin leaders, not only in Peru but in other Latin
American nations.   In contrast to other Peruvian parties,
the APRA was not organized to struggle for limited
governmental power among articulate elites to the ex-
clusion of a majority of the population, the Indian and
mestizo masses.   Returning from exile, Haya ran for
president of Peru in 1931 and lost.   Then in 1936, the
Apristas were suppressed and did not return to public
life until 1945.   In 1946, three Apristas became cabinet
Ministers, but in 1948 the party was again outlawed.
Legalized again in 1956, APRA began to stress nation-
alistic goals in contrast to its earlier vision as a movement for all of Latin America, and to stress its newer
orientation the group became the Partido Aprista Peruano, or PAP.   After a 31-year lapse, Haya was again
a presidential candidate in 1962.   The results of the
1962 election were nullified and the same candidates
ran again in June 1963, with Haya losing to Fernando
Belaúnde of the Popular Action party.   When the military took power in October 1968, all parties were suspended.   With elections announced for 1978 to choose a
100-seat Constituent Assembly to draft constitutional
changes for the suspended Constitution of 1933, political
party activity revived in 1977.   On November 16, 1977,
a new Electoral Law promulgated the guidelines for the
1978 election and for the anticipated 1980 general elec-

tions.   As of 1978, the Apristas found themselves the
largest political party in Peru, as had been the case a
few times in the 1960s.

ALLIANCE FOR PROGRESS.   The Alianza para el Progreso
was originally suggested by Brazilian President Jusce-
lino Kubitschek in 1958 as "Operation Pan America."
U.S. President John F. Kennedy renamed it in March
1961 as the Alliance at the suggestion of Senator Hubert
Humphrey.   On August 17, 1961, at Punta del Este,
Uruguay, all Latin American nations except Cuba joined
the United States in signing the Alliance charter, setting
up a ten-year program.   Each Latin American nation
drafted specific plans for modernizing and expanding its
economy and for instituting social reforms.   Because
Peru during 1965-1968 increasingly pressured the International Petroleum Company (a Standard Oil of New Jersey subsidiary) to sell to the Peruvian public and private
investors, the U.S. did not implement all of Peru's requests for Alliance loans.   In October 1968, Peru expropriated IPC and in 1969 amicably reached a settlement payment with IPC.   Then the outstanding Alliance
loans were finalized.

AMAZONAS.   One of the 24 Departments into which the republic is divided for administrative purposes.   The Department of the Amazonas is subdivided into five Provinces.

AMPATO.   A mountain peak located approximately halfway
between the cities of Arequipa and Puno in southern
Peru.   It rises to 21,000 feet (6,300 meters) above sea
level, one of the highest peaks of the Andes in southern
Peru.

ANCASH.   One of the 24 Departments of the republic of Peru.
The Department of Ancash is subdivided into sixteen
Provinces.

ANCON.   The town of Ancón lies thirty-five kilometers north
of Lima, on the coast.   It was the site of the signing
of the treaty in 1883 which ended Peru's war with Chile.
In modern times, Ancón has served as the site for a
major installation of the Inter-American Geodetic Commission.   A team of United States scientists from a
special geodetic survey team used Ancón throughout the
1950s as a global benchmark in measuring the exact cur-

vature of the earth's surface, yielding data which were
subsequently utilized in mapping the coastlines of the
Western Hemisphere and the coastal shelf of the Pacific
Ocean.

ANCON, TREATY OF (1883). In the War of the Pacific, Peru
and its ally, Bolivia, were defeated in various battles in
1879, and Chile militarily occupied the provinces of
Tacna, Arica, and Tarapacá. Under the Treaty of Ancón, Peru lost Tarapacá to Chile permanently, and lost
Tacna and Arica, regions rich in nitrates, for at least
ten years. Hence the nitrate revenues the Peruvian
treasury needed badly at the time to bolster an economy
injured by the War of the Pacific were no longer avail-
able. The modern boundary line between Peru and Chile
finds Arica as Chile's most northern city and Tacna as
Peru's most southern city, with the Department of Tacna
the southernmost of Peru's twenty-four departments.
After the shock of the War of the Pacific and Chilean
occupation, General Miguel Iglesias became provisional
President of Peru. After Chilean troops marched into
Lima in January 1881, President Nicolás de Piérola had
become incoherent and moved his government to Ayacucho, where Congress deserted him. In October 1883,
a rump Congress agreed to the Treaty of Ancón. General Iglesias, as provisional President, assumed the
distasteful task of signing the Ancón Treaty, and thereafter found himself denounced as a traitor by Peruvian
troops still armed in the hinterlands.

ANDEAN COMMON MARKET. Also called the Andean Pact,
this multinational organization has its headquarters in
Lima. In addition to Peru, the other republics of the
Andean region--Colombia, Ecuador, Bolivia, and Chile
--signed an agreement in 1966 to integrate economically
on a subregional basis. These republics were already
members of the larger Latin American Free Trade Association, which had been formed in 1960 to integrate
all of the South American republics. After the Andean
Pact organization began to reduce a few tariffs among
its member nations, in 1973 Venezuela decided to join,
but in 1976 Venezuela withdrew from the Andean Pact
to promote its own newer concept launched in 1975, the
Latin American Economic System (Sistema Económico
de Latino América; SELA), with headquarters in Caracas.

ANGULO, JOSE and VICENTE. The Angulo brothers became

the second and third in command under Mateo García
Pumacahua in August 1814 in Cuzco, in the first major
attack by Peruvians for independence against Spanish
forces. The Angulo brothers and García Pumacahua then
marched on Arequipa and captured it in December 1814,
before Viceroy Abascal could concentrate sufficient troops
there. Early in 1815, however, Abascal's Spanish forces
outnumbered the 5,000 Peruvian independence forces and
defeated the rebels.   Not until 1821 did Peru drive out
Spanish troops permanently.

APURIMAC.   One of the 24 Departments or basic administrative units of the republic.   The word "Apurímac" was
used in the Inca Empire at the time the Spaniards came
to Peru in 1533 in the Quechua language to denote the
princely estates of the children of the Inca Emperor,
located west and south of the Inca capital of Cuzco.   The
Department of Apurímac contains six Provinces.

AREQUIPA.   The name of the second largest city of Peru,
which is the capital of the Department of the same name.
The 1972 Census reported the city of Arequipa as having
a population of 235,000, and the Department of the Arequipa as having 390,000 inhabitants.   Peru's population
throughout the 1970s was increasing at the rate of 3.2
per cent annually.

ATAHUALPA.   In 1526 the Emperor of the Inca Empire,
Huayna Capac, died of a pestilence before he could name
his heir to the crown.   His elder son, Huáscar, took
power in Cuzco, ruling what is today Bolivia (then called
Upper Peru because of its towering mountain peaks) and
much of Peru.   Atahualpa, the half brother of Huáscar,
was Huayna Capac's son by the late Inca ruler's second
wife, whereas Huáscar's mother had been Huayna's principal wife or Empress.   Atahualpa, therefore, took power
in Quito, ruling over what today represents Ecuador and
a small northern portion of Peru.   Soon Atahualpa and
Huáscar were at war, fighting to take each other's part
of the fragmented kingdom, each half-brother claiming
sole right to Huayna's total Inca Empire.   In 1532, just
as the invading Spaniards penetrated the interior regions
of Peru, Huáscar was captured and sent to be humiliated
and tortured by Atahualpa's officers, at Atahualpa's military command post in the city of Cajamarca.   Then,
suddenly, Francisco Pizarro used his European weapons
--the firepower of guns and cannons--to subdue both fac-

tions of Indians, ending the independence of both Inca
Empires.   Peru became a Spanish colony, later to bear
the title of Viceroyalty of Peru.

AYACUCHO.   One of Peru's 24 Departments, subdivided into
seven Provinces.

AYACUCHO, BATTLE OF.   On December 9, 1824, ensued
the famed battle near the town of Ayacucho, halfway between Lima and Cuzco.   General Antonio José Sucre, a
Venezuelan-born leader of Peruvian troops and only 32
years of age, commanded 5,700 soldiers against 9,300
Spanish troops commanded by the Viceroy himself, General José de la Serna.   More than 1,600 soldiers of
Spain were killed, whereas only 300 Peruvian troops
were lost.   Spain's colonial empire in the Americas,
after three centuries of unchallenged authority and a
decade of battles, was now at an end, except for the
islands of Cuba and Puerto Rico, awaiting their own
break with the motherland in 1898.   Ayacucho symbol-
izes not only the last battle in Peru before the final de-
parture of the Spaniards, but also the official end of
Spain's mainland empire in the Americas, begun in 1492.

AYLLU.   In the Inca Empire before the conquest by Spain,
the ayllu was the basic kin group of Quechua or Aymará
Indians.   Each ayllu was governed by a man of fairness
and ability, chosen for his leadership rather than his
aristocratic heritage.   The ayllu chief's job was the
basic means of upward mobility in an Inca society other-
wise rigidly based on class, with authority coming from
above and duty to the community and empire from below.
Foremen within each ayllu were ruled by a Curaca, with
the curacas of each Inca province governed by a Governor.   The Inca realm was administratively divided into
four regions, each governed by a Prefect.   When the
Inca Emperor needed any information about any ayllu in
the empire, he asked the appropriate Prefect, who in
turn asked the appropriate Governor, who consulted the
appropriate Curaca, who knew the public life of his ayllu
from daily economic activities to social life.   Spanish
conquerers were able to impose an autocratic European
colonial viceregal administration on top of this Inca governmental hierarchy.   The disciplined ayllu helped the
Spaniards conquer the native Peruvians from the top
downward.

AYMARA.   The name of the indigenous Indians making up the
    second largest linguistic and cultural group within the
    Inca Empire.   During three centuries of Spanish colon-
    ialism and independence of nation-states since the 1820s,
    the cultural differences between the Aymarás and the
    Quechuas remain discernible.   Today more Aymarás
    live in Bolivia than in southern Peru, where their cul-
    tural cousins, the Quechuas remain the largest Indian
    group, as in the pre-Hispanic era.

-B-

BALTA, JOSE.   In January 1868, Colonel José Balta, an of-
    ficer of the Corps of Engineers and a conservative po-
    litical leader, led a coup d'état against President Mar-
    iano Ignacio Prado, and took over the government.   He
    set aside Prado's liberal Constitution of 1867 and Pra-
    do's anti-clerical decrees designed to curb the power of
    the Catholic bishops in governmental policy formulation.
    Restoring the conservative Constitution of 1860, Balta
    remained in power for a full presidential term, 1868-
    1872.   His Minister of Finance, Nicolás de Piérola, a
    man who would figure prominently in Peruvian politics
    for half a century, believed the public debt to be unman-
    ageable, and in 1869 had French capitalists take charge
    of marketing Peru's fertilizer industry of two million
    tons of guano exports annually.   The new income reduced
    the foreign debt and permitted President Balta to begin
    Peru's railroad age, getting American engineer Henry
    Meiggs to construct tracks high in the Andes, which
    connected heretofore isolated provincial cities with the
    coast.

BAMBA see PAMPA

BASADRE, JORGE.   Born in Tacna on February 12, 1903.
    Son of Carlos Basadre and Olga Grohmann de Basadre.
    Graduated from Colegio Alemán in Lima, then the Cole-
    gio de Guadalupe.   Attended National University of San
    Marcos, receiving the degrees of Litt. D. and LL. D.
    Professor of history at the Faculty of Letters of San
    Marcos University since 1928 and member of the Fac-
    ulty of Law of San Marcos University since 1931.   Di-
    rector of the Library of the University of San Marcos
    during 1930-1931 and 1935-1942.   Visiting Scholar of
    Library Science of Carnegie Foundation in the United

States, 1931-1932. Scholar, Ibero-American Institution of Berlin, 1932. Professor, Centro de Estudios of University of Sevilla, Spain, 1933. Editor of Boletín Bibliográfico since 1936. Secretary General of Congress of Americanists in Lima, 1939. Professor, Faculty of Letters, University of Buenos Aires, 1942. Minister of Public Education in presidential cabinet, 1945. Director of Biblioteca Nacional del Perú. Member of Academia Peruana de la Lengua, Sociedad de Historia de Chile, Academía de la Historia de Argentina, Société des Americainistes de Paris. Author of La iniciación de la república, 2 volumes, 1928-30; La multitud, la ciudad y el campo en la historia del Perú, 1929; Perú: problema y posibilidad, 1931; Historia del derecho peruano, 1937; Historia de la república del Perú, 1939-1970, 19 volumes. (See the Bibliography under IX. History; B. Since Independence.)

BELAUNDE TERRY, FERNANDO. Born in Lima on October 7, 1912. Married to Carola Aubry (divorced), and in April 1970 to Violeta Correa Miller; two children. Graduated from the University of Texas at Austin in 1935 with a B.S. in architecture and a professional architect's license. Joined the Club Nacional in 1938. Deputy in Congress, 1945-1948. Dean of Faculty of Architecture, National Engineering University, Lima, 1955-1960. Founded the Popular Action (Acción Popular) political party in 1956 and was AP candidate for President in the elections of 1956, 1962 and 1963. The military leaders took power after a three-way stalemated election in June 1962, with a Junta governing for one year. In June 1963, the same three candidates again vied for the presidency. AP candidate Belaúnde defeated Aprista candidate Víctor Raúl Haya de la Torre and National Odriísta Union candidate Manuel Odría. Belaúnde took office July 28, 1963, for a six-year term ending July 28, 1969, but on October 3, 1968 he was ousted by a military coup d'état, and he took up exile residence in the United States. In May 1977, he returned to Lima to help reorganize his party for the anticipated 1978 and 1980 elections. He planned to modernize Peru through large public works and moderate economic and social reforms. Belaúnde's goals were blocked by an opposition Congress and the wealthy leaders of the banking and plantation sectors of the economy.

BELTRAN, PEDRO. Publisher of the Lima daily newspaper

La Prensa until the military government of President
Juan Velasco expropriated it.   Beltrán had served as
the chief cabinet minister for President Manuel Prado
during 1959-1962, and symbolized traditional political
opposition to the social reform expropriation of busi-
nesses and agricultural holdings pushed by the military
leaders who took power in October 1968.   La Prensa's
criticism of General Velasco's government continued under the press freedom which obtained in Peru until the
military government promulgated the so-called "Press
Freedom Statute" by decree on January 9, 1970.   This
law states that a Peruvian publisher must not remain
out of the country more than six months in any one year.
Beltrán left Peru on July 10, 1971, to serve as a Visiting Professor of Economics at the University of Virginia,
and returned to Lima on January 21, 1972.   An order
removing Beltrán as publisher stated that the residence
requirement does not take into consideration solely the
calendar year.   On April 6, 1972, Beltrán had to sell
his 50,504 shares of stock to the 508 employees of La
Prensa.   His nephew, Pedro Beltrán Balén replaced his
uncle as interim publisher.   On March 18, 1972, Beltrán the younger was fined 2,110 dollars for reporting
about the Peruvian ambassador to Mexico in a manner
the government ruled was libelous.   Under a 1974 presidential decree, La Prensa was expropriated by the government and turned over to a workers' group.   As with
all other Peruvian newspapers with circulations of 20,000
or more, La Prensa, on July 29, 1974, was classified
as "social property" and title to the newspaper was given
to the Industrial Workers Civil Association.   But the
publicized plan of the Velasco government to insure that
each workers' group in society would eventually have its
own editorial voice in daily journalism was nullified in
practice because the government continued to designate
the executive publisher of each newspaper, thereby in-
suring that the daily press would not be so critical of
the government that unlawful overthrow of that government might be engendered.   After August 1975, the administration of President Fernando Morales Bermúdez
slowly eased governmental "guidance" of the mass media,
tightening and loosening control as crises prompted.   But
the days of the private publisher epitomized by Pedro
Beltrán seemed over, even as Peru prepared to elect
a civilian government in 1980.

BENAVIDES, OSCAR R. (1876-1945).   When President of Peru

Luis Sánchez Cerro was assassinated on April 30, 1933
by an Aprista, Congress elected as acting President of
Peru General Oscar R.   Benavides, a representative of
the creole oligarchy, the so-called "Forty Families"
(perhaps a few hundred families in practice) who owned
the largest plantations, ranches, and farms in the republic.   President Benavides tried to heal the breach
between the Apristas and the military-oligarchy political
leadership by releasing Aprista leader Víctor Raúl Haya
de la Torre from prison.   Benavides created a Ministry
of Public Health and Welfare, to provide basic services
to the poor.   He canceled the results of the election of
1936 while the vote tabulation was in progress, extending
his own presidency with the backing of the army.   In
1939, Benavides helped civilian Manuel Prado win a six-
year presidential term, from July 28, 1939 to July 28,
1945.

BENAVIDES BENAVIDES, JOSE.   Born on May 21, 1920, in
Lima, the son of former President Oscar R. Benavides.
Graduated at the head of his class from the Escuela
Militar de Chorrillos in 1940 and commissioned in the
infantry.   Graduate studies at the French Military Academy at St. Cyr and at the U.S. Infantry Command Course
at Fort Benning, Georgia.   Also the U.S. Armored Command School at Fort Knox, Kentucky.   In 1966, he became Chief of Army Intelligence.   Prefect of the Department of Loreto, headquartered in Iquitos, 1967 and 1968.
Minister of Agriculture from October 3, 1968, to June
12, 1969.   Then Envoy of the Peruvian agricultural mission to Egypt, then to Israel.   Director of Logistics for
the Army, 1970-1977.

BILLINGHURST, GUILLERMO.   In 1903, Billinghurst was a
rival of Nicolás de Piérola for the leadership of the
Democratic Party.   By 1912, Billinghurst had gained
control of the Democratic Party, Piérola having faltered
less than a year before his death.   Billinghurst was a
millionaire business executive whose paternal grandfather,
an Englishman, had married a Peruvian aristocratic lady.
Billinghurst believed that the survival of a republican
form of government in Peru depended upon the survival
of capitalism and that both depended upon reforms of
benefit more to the working class than to aristocrats.
He proposed broadening the base of the electorate and
creating modern labor legislation.   Thus, although a
wealthy member of the élite, Billinghurst proclaimed a

program discernibly progressive, projecting an image
of a social liberal combined with a fiscal conservative.
Billinghurst found himself to be genuinely popular with
the working class voters, yet some of his partisans
wrecked certain polling places in the belief that a smaller
turnout on election day would obviate a popular majority
vote, throwing the election to Congress, where Billinghurst could win an Electoral College balloting.   May 25,
1912, proved to be chaotic, indeed, and Congress nullified the results.   Congress then elected Billinghurst,
who was inaugurated on September 24, 1912.   His labor
programs enraged Congress and on February 4, 1914,
troops under Colonel Oscar R. Benavides ousted Billinghurst from the presidential palace.

BINGHAM, HIRAM.   Born in Honolulu, Hawaii, on November
19, 1875.   Died in June 1956.   Discoverer of the Peruvian lost city of the Incas, Machu Picchu in 1911.   Graduated from Yale in 1898.   Ph. D. from Harvard in 1905.
Honorary Doctor of Letters from the University of Cuzco
in 1912.   Taught history and political science at Harvard
during 1901-1905 and at Princeton 1905-1906.   Explored
Bolívar's route across Venezuela and Colombia 1906-
1907.   U. S. delegate to Pan American Scientific Congress
in Santiago de Chile in 1908.   Explored Spanish colonial
trade route from Buenos Aires to Lima during 1909.
Director of the Yale Peruvian Expedition during 1911,
discovering Machu Picchu high in the Andes of Cuzco
Department.   Also scaled Mount Corpuna to 21,703 feet
for the National Geographic Society.   Professor of Latin
American history at Yale University, 1915-1924.   Con-
necticut Lieutenant Governor, Governor, and Senator,
1923-1933.   Editor of National Aero Magazine 1933-1935.
Member Lima Geographical Society, Peruvian Academy
of History, Venezuelan Academy of History.   Author of
Vitcos, Last Inca Capital, 1912; Inca Land, 1922; Machu
Picchu, 1930; and Lost City of the Incas: The Story of
Machu Picchu and Its Builders, 1948, reprinted 1963.

BLANCO, HUGO.   Born in 1941 in Cuzco.   Studied agronomy.
Although both his father and mother's families, the Blanco
and Gladós lineage, were of a Spanish-Indian (mestizo)
admixture for generations, for political purposes in organizing Indians, Blanco has claimed to be a Quechua
in many political rallies, using fragmentary Quechuan
phrases.   By the time he reached his teenage, Blanco
had become a dedicated Trotskyite Marxist, pledged to

bloody revolution to destroy Peruvian society and rebuild
it as a Marxist nation. In the Introduction to his book,
Land or Death, published in English in 1972, Blanco's
lieutenants state flatly that the volume is polemic propaganda, yet groups sponsoring Blanco's lecture tour of
the United States in 1977 advertised it as a "documentary
of the peasant struggle." At university campuses in 97
American cities, Blanco was identified in advertisements
as an "exiled peasant leader." No mention during his
U.S. tour was made by his sponsors of his confession
and conviction of killing two policemen and being offered
exile in lieu of prison. Blanco has served as Secretary
General of the Revolutionary Workers Party, the Peruvian affiliate of the Fourth International or global confederation of Trotskyite parties. In 1958, Blanco, still
in his teens, organized the peasants of the Convención
Valley of Cuzco into 150 unions, grouped into a peasant
federation. After the unions seized lands in 1960, army
troops began ousting them. In 1963, national police captured Blanco, but not before he killed two police officers.
An international campaign by Marxists and leftist sym-
pathizers flooded mass media and academic journals of
the Western Hemisphere with pleas for Blanco, and after almost eight years in prison, he was freed, on con-
dition that he go into exile. Blanco has resided in Cuba,
Mexico, and Argentina. After his 1977 lecture tour of
the United States, he settled in Jujuy, in Argentina, to
campaign by mail and tape recordings for the June 18,
1978, election in Peru of 100 members of a Constituent
Assembly. His new group, the Popular, Student, Peasant, and Worker Front (Frente Obrero, Campesino, Es-
tudantíl y Popular; FOCEP) won 12 per cent of the vote
or 12 seats, one of which went to Blanco.

BOLIVAR, SIMON.   Born on July 24, 1783, in Caracas, Ven-
    ezuela.   Died of tuberculosis on December 17, 1830, in
    Santa Marta, Colombia.   His parents had been aristo-
    crats, creoles (Spaniards born in the New World).   Or-
    phaned at age nine, he was reared by an uncle, who
    sent him to Madrid in 1799 to complete his education.
    At age eighteen, Bolívar married María de Toro.   In
    1802, they settled in Caracas, where his young wife soon
    died.   In 1804 he visited Napoleon in France and scien-
    tist Alexander von Humboldt in Germany, being convinced
    by both that South America was ripe for independence
    from Spain.   He joined the junta which overthrew the
    Spanish colonial government in Caracas on April 19, 1810.

In 1811, Bolívar became a general in Colombia and liberated Venezuela from the Spanish in 1813.   He again
defeated the Spanish in Colombia in 1819.   In 1822 he
helped General Antonio de Sucre defeat Spanish troops
in Ecuador.   In 1823, Bolívar entered Peru with an army
which won other battles against Spanish troops.   In December 1824, he helped Peru win the battle of Ayacucho.
Bolívar went on to liberate neighboring Upper Peru,
which was renamed Bolivia in his honor.

BUSTAMANTE, JOSE.   José Luis Bustamante was elected
President of Peru in 1945 at the close of President Manuel Prado's six-year term, in an open and free election.
Bustamante was the candidate of a democratic coalition
of parties, including the Apristas.   Bustamante appointed
Apristas as three of his cabinet ministers.   In January
1947 a conservative Lima newspaper publisher was mur-
dered and President Bustamante put the blame on the
Apristas.   His three Aprista ministers resigned from
his administration and enough members of the Senate
boycotted legislative sessions to prevent a quorum.   Legislation was blocked.   After acts of violence in the port
city of Callao in 1948 by Apristas, Bustamante outlawed
the APRA.   In November 1948, General Manuel Odría
removed Bustamante from office, sent him into exile in
Argentina, and assumed the presidency himself.

-C-

CABILDO.   A cabildo or town council was an entity brought
to Peru by Spanish colonial administrators.   After Francisco Pizarro completed the conquest of the Inca Empire
for Spain in 1533, he organized on paper Peru's first
cabildo, and after founding Lima on January 6, 1535,
proclaimed that the new city had replaced the ancient
Inca capital of Cuzco as the capital of Peru.   Lima
would contain the seat of the Viceroyalty and, in addition, a cabildo to handle only local matters.   Spain itself had a modest tradition of urban government from
Roman times, and after the reconquest of Spain from
the Moors, the concept of a municipal council was re-
kindled.   The only self-government the Kings of Spain
encouraged in three centuries of colonial rule in Peru
was the town council.   Thus, when the fighting for independence from Spain began in Peru after 1810, the
only Peruvians with European-style administrative ex-

perience in limited self-government were the members
of cabildos. Peruvian cabildos had rarely ever challenged any order of any viceroy, for most members of
cabildos, called regidores (council members), were
landed gentry or high-ranking military officers, themselves part of the royal establishment in the New World.
The cabildo, even before independence from Spain, however, did develop into the only political forum in Peru
in which American-born Spaniards, or creoles, could
challenge some of privileges assumed by the peninsulares,
or Spaniards born in Spain who came to Peru to dominate public life.

CACERES, ANDRES. General Andrés A. Cáceres entered
Lima in November 1885 to bring order out of chaos in
the aftermath of Peru's defeat by Chile in the War of
the Pacific. Cáceres remained in power as President
of Peru from 1885 to 1890, longer than the four-year
term specified in the Constitution of 1860. As a national
military hero, Cáceres was able to symbolize Peruvian
national pride and help citizens recover from the blow
to their pride of having Chile take territory away from
Peru by force. Cáceres organized the Constitutionalist
Party to encourage civilian leadership to intermingle
with his fellow officers, trying to govern and guide Peru
out of the economic depths brought on by war debts.

CADE. A widely-used acronym in Peruvian newspapers for
Conferencia Anual de Ejecutivos (Annual Conference of
Executives). Begun in 1961, the 1976 CADE drew 620
representatives from all private and public sectors of
Peruvian public life.

CAEM. The Centro de Altos Estudios Militares (Center for
Higher Military Studies), or CAEM, was founded in 1958
in Chorrillos, a suburb south of Lima, adjacent to the
Escuela Militar, the college which prepares young cadets
to become commissioned officers in the Army. By contrast, the CAEM has for its student body Army colonels,
with eight per cent of its openings reserved for Air
Force colonels, eight per cent for Navy captains, and
approximately 10 to 30 per cent of its students being
civilian administrators of the national government since
1969, depending on the year and the needs of the nation's
public administration corps. Each colonel or other student at CAEM of equivalent naval, police, or civil-ser-
vice rank is given a one-year course stressing public

administration, economics, and national planning. CAEM
has become the "think tank" for high-level public policy
formulation in Peru, and the gateway for colonels to become generals and captains to become admirals.

CAJAMARCA. One of the 24 Departments into which Peru is
divided geographically for administrative purposes. It
contains 11 Provinces.

CALDERON, PEDRO JOSE. The editor in 1878 of the pro-
clerical newspaper La Patria. His editorials attacking
former Peruvian President Manuel Pardo, then a Senator, inflamed mobs against Pardo, who had been cor-
rectly warning Peru of an impending attack by Chile.
Pardo was assassinated on November 16, 1878; since
September, Calderón had been openly calling for Pardo's
death.

CALICHE. Mineral salt found just below the surface of the
soil of Peru. Used to manufacture nitrate of soda as
a fertilizer (see GUANO).

CALLAO. A Province with the constitutional status of a Department and administered as the twenty-fourth Department of the republic. This province contains the port
city of Callao, which serves as the port for adjacent
Lima. In recent decades, all vacant lands between
downtown Callao and downtown Lima have been developed
into industrial sites and residential areas. Passengers
on city buses serving the greater Lima metropolitan area
are often unaware when they cross the municipal boundary lines separating Lima and Callao.

CANDAMO, MANUEL. Active in the Civilista Party, Candamo in 1902 attracted public attention as an energetic
president of the Lima Chamber of Commerce. He became a candidate for President of Peru in 1903 and won,
being inaugurated in November. But he died of illness
after only eight months in office, in July 1904.

CANGALLO, BATTLE OF. On April 5, 1834, at Cangallo,
constitutionalist forces commanded by General Domingo
Nieto were defeated by troops commanded by General
Miguel San Román, who opposed constitutionally-elected
Luís José de Orbegoso's being inaugurated as President
of Peru. Later many of the San Román troops deserted
to Nieto and Orbegoso could function as Chief Executive
of the government.

CARETAS. Founded in 1950, Caretas, published twice a
month, soon became the leading news magazine in Peru.
It offered in-depth reporting about national problems and
succeeded in constructively criticizing President Manual
Prado during 1956-1962 and President Fernando Belaúnde
during 1963-1968. In November 1968, the military government of President Juan Velasco censored Caretas,
then forced it to suspend publication. With the easing
of controls over the media after General Francisco Morales Bermúdez became president in 1975, Caretas began to recover its status as an organ of national life under surrogate publisher Doris Gibson Parra. By 1977,
publisher Enrique Zileri had been allowed to return from
exile. The magazine's writers in the late 1970s included
Peru's distinguished novelist Mario Vargas Llosa and
essayist-commentator Luis Alberto Sánchez, who had,
as president (rector) of San Marcos University, helped
modernize Peru's university curricula.

CASTILLA, RAMON. Elected President of Peru in April 1845.
Ramón Castilla, the constitutional president who governed
Peru longer than any other 19th-century chief executive,
was born in 1799. As Minister of the Treasury during
President Augustín Gamarra's second term (1839-1841),
Castilla helped initiate a steamship service to Peruvian
ports. Castilla contrasted with the majority of Peruvian
leaders of his time, who were Spanish in ethnic origin;
his mother was an Indian and his appearance was Quechuan, not Spanish, symbolizing the ascendancy of a few
indigenous leaders into Peruvian public life, after more
than three centuries of colonial, then republican, leaders who were white rather than hybrid (mestizo or cholo).
During his first term (1845-1851), President Castilla
stressed in several announcements that his priorities
were headed by a commitment to establishing civil law
and order. He used the army as a constabulary force
to prevent regional leaders in remote provincial regions
from operating their own fiefdoms in defiance of the national government. He built up a modest amount of public support by organizing a bipartisan advisory committee
of liberals and conservatives. On October 21, 1845,
Castilla sent to Congress the first national budget ever
prepared in Peruvian history. His second term (1855-
1862) saw the promulgation of the Constitution of 1860,
and not only recognized Catholicism as the nation's official religion but also prohibited the public practice of
any other religion. This prohibition remained in effect
until removed by constitutional amendment in 1915.

CHAVIN see INCA

CHICLAYO. A port city in northern Peru, 275 kilometers
    south of the Ecuador-Peru border. Chiclayo functioned
    principally as a port of call for small fishing fleets from
    the 1860s to the 1960s, when it began increasingly to
    serve the oil-exploration crews prospecting for petroleum
    in the northern jungle.

CHIMBOTE. A port town 230 kilometers north of Lima,
    which served as a harbor for Quechua fishing rafts dur-
    ing the Inca Empire. Since 1958, Chimbote has been
    a facility for fishing fleets and a transhipment point for
    small fish destined to be used in the manufacture of
    fishmeal.

CHINCHA. A small port town 95 kilometers south of Lima,
    which has given its name to the beer Indians have brewed
    from fermented corn since the days of the Inca Empire,
    corrupted to "chicha."

CHOCANO, JOSE. Peru's celebrated poet of the 1920s, who
    went to Mexico in 1915 to join the revolutionary troops
    of Pancho Villa. Upon his return to Lima, Chocano
    published a book in 1922, Apuntes sobre las dictaduras
    organizadoras, which surprised the literary elite of Latin
    America because it defended the policies of Augusto B.
    Leguía, whose presidency in Peru (1919-1930) was widely
    considered to be a dictatorship.

CHOLO see MESTIZO

CHORRILLOS. A town within the greater metropolitan area
    of Lima, just south of the suburb of Miraflores, and
    home of the Escuela Militar, which educates cadets to
    become commissioned officers in the army. Adjacent
    to the military college is the Center for Higher Military
    Studies, the apex of graduate studies for career officers
    (see CAEM).

CHRISTIAN DEMOCRATIC PARTY. The Partido Demócrata-
    Cristiano, or PDC, was founded in Peru as a modern
    party in 1955 by Héctor Cornejo Chávez, but in political
    philosophy traces its origin back to the Catholic civic
    groups of the 1940s. In 1956 the PDC did not have its
    own presidential candidate but supported the candidacy
    of Popular Action's Fernando Belaúnde. The PDC did

win more congressional seats than the other major political parties. The PDC's strength centered in Arequipa, but it began to grow in Lima, Puno, Mollendo,
and Trujillo. For the June 1963 election the PDC formed
an official coalition with Popular Action, supporting and
helping Belaúnde to win the presidency. In the Senate
and in the Chamber of Deputies, the PDC and the Popular Action members of Congress functioned as an inte-
grated coalition, with both parties voting as one from
1963 to early 1968, when the PDC and President Belaúnde's Popular Action Senators and Deputies began to
split on major issues. On October 3, 1968, a military
government took power and suspended Congress and political parties. In 1977, the PDC and other parties were
again legalized, in preparation for the scheduled election
of June 4, 1978, to select 100 members of a Constituent
Assembly, and for the anticipated 1980 elections of a
Congress and a civilian President. The PDC's ideology
is based on Catholic social reforms growing out of Pope
John's two papal encyclicals of 1963, Mater et Magistra
and Pacem in Terris.

CISNEROS, ANTONIO. Recognized internationally as Peru's
    leading poet in the 1960s and 1970s, Antonio Cisneros
    was born in Lima on December 27, 1942. He received
    his doctorate in literature from the National University
    of San Marcos in 1974. He has taught literature at uni-
    versities in England, France, and Hungary, and is a
    professor at San Marcos. His Comentarios reales,
    which won the 1965 National Poetry Prize, portrayed
    Peruvian historical experiences. His Canto ceremonial
    won the 1968 poetry prize in the Cuban Casa de las
    Américas. Two volumes of his poems were translated
    into English and published in 1970 in London as The
    Spider.

CIVILISTAS. Members of the Civilista Party formed Peru's
    first full-scale modern political party, the Civilianist
    Party, and called themselves civilistas, opponents of
    military government. The party began in 1871 and fielded
    its first candidates in 1872. By 1924, it had withered
    away.

COMENTARIOS REALES. A detailed description of Indian
    life in Peru before the conquest by the Spaniards, writ-
    ten by Garcilaso de la Vega, son of a Spanish conqueror
    and an Indian mother who was from an Inca family of

nobility.   Garcilaso was popularly known as "El Inca"
and became the most famous mestizo (Spanish-Indian
hybrid) of the colonial period.   Born in 1539, he wrote
the Comentarios reales in his old age and became a valuable source for modern historians seeking perspective
on a pre-Hispanic culture, government, and economics.
His Royal Commentaries provide first-hand description
by a knowledgeable and intelligent bilingual analyst of
such entities of governmental administration under the
Inca as the local social unit called the ayllu (see AYLLU).

COMERCIO, EL.   The Lima daily El Comercio, the oldest
    newspaper in Peru, is the second oldest newspaper in
    all of Latin America, having been founded in 1839 (El
    Mercurio of Valparaiso, Chile, founded in 1827, is the
    oldest).   Its first issue (Vol. 1, No. 1, May 4, 1839)
    proclaimed that El Comercio would be dedicated to "or-
    der, liberty, knowledge."   Until 1970, the morning daily
    paper kept faith with that promise, supporting public or-
    der when threatened by violence, stressing 19th-century
    liberalism of the rugged-individual archetype, and later
    evolving into 20th-century political conservatism.   As
    its very name, "Commerce," implies, financial news
    always received special emphasis in El Comercio.   Edi-
    torially, until the 1970s, it supported policies favorable
    to the exporters, the land-owning wealthy families.   When
    the progressive military government began to pressure
    the press with a 1970 Press Law, El Comercio began
    to self-censor itself, avoiding criticism of the social
    revolution General Juan Velasco's government had launched
    in October 1968.   But the end of a conservative editor-
    ial stance and even mild support for the military reform-
    ers did not save El Comercio from being expropriated.
    Like all other Peruvian daily newspapers, El Comercio
    was declared to be "social property" under a 1974 de-
    cree.   Throughout the remainder of the 1970s, as the
    1980 election of a civilian government drew near, the
    government-chosen executive publisher remained in charge,
    even though technically the title of ownership of this
    prominent newspaper in 1977 and 1978 indicated that a
    workers' society or interest group "owned" it.   That
    group of farm workers includes ranch hands.

COMISION INTERMINISTERIAL.   The Comisión Interminis-
    terial was created by President Fernando Belaúnde in
    1963, and functioned into 1968.   The Commission con-
    sisted of the Undersecretaries of the key cabinet min-

istries, who met monthly to formulate policies for the
Commission Volunteers, a group of young Peruvians pat-
terned after the Vista Volunteers in the United States
and partly inspired by the U.S. Peace Corps Volunteers.
The Interministerial Commission Volunteers worked in
the impoverished neighborhoods of Lima, Callao, Arequipa, Cuzco, Puno, and Mollendo for brief periods,
trying to teach basic job skills and basic sanitation and
public health standards.   In the 1970s, the military government continued a limited version of the Commission
Volunteers by assigning low-level employees to work with
residents of the "pueblos jóvenes," or new-town slums,
coordinated by the National Mobilization Service (see
SINAMOS).

COMMUNIST PARTY.   The Peruvian Communist Party (Par-
    tido Comunista Peruano; PCP) had its origins in the
    Peruvian Socialist Party founded by José Carlos Mariá-
    tegui in 1928.   The party took its present name in 1930.
    Since 1964, the movement has been divided into a pro-
    Soviet Union party and several pro-Chinese groups, two
    of which also use the PCP name, usually with an extra
    word of qualification in parenthesis.   Throughout the
    1960s and 1970s, there also functioned in Peru the Cas-
    tro-oriented or pro-Cuban Revolutionary Leftist Move-
    ment (Movimiento de Izquierda Revolucionaria; MIR).
    The MIR has advocated violence and political murder,
    in contrast to the superficial co-existence the Soviet-
    line PCP has publicly preached.   The highest organ of
    the pro-Soviet PCP is its National Congress, which is
    supposed to meet every three years.   Its Sixth Congress
    met in November 1973; its Seventh was postponed indef-
    initely in 1976.   However, in 1976 and 1977, seventeen
    regional and local PCP conferences were held.   The
    government decided in November 1977 that the PCP
    would be recognized as a legal party for the 1978 and
    1980 elections.   Throughout the 1970s, the PCP secre-
    tary general was Jorge del Prado.   The PCP's youth
    group, Peruvian Communist Youth (Juventud Comunista
    Peruana; JCP), has operated throughout the universities,
    striving to put JCP members in charge of as many stu-
    dent federation offices as possible.   JCP students vigor-
    ously support any faculty members in any Peruvian uni-
    versity known to be Marxists or sympathetic to Marxists
    and, conversely, demonstrate publicly against various
    known anti-Marxist professors.   A major source of the
    PCP's influence in Peruvian public life throughout the

1970s has been its control of the General Federation of Workers of Peru, the largest federation of labor unions in the republic.

CONACO. Corporación Nacional de Comerciantes, or CONACO, the National Merchants Association, since 1963 has spoken for one big sector of organized management in public dialogues, lobbying with appropriate entities of government to point out the needs of Peru's merchant class. From October 1968 through August 1975, under the administration of President Juan Velasco, the Peruvian government tended to ignore the suggestions and requests of CONACO. Since September 1975, the government of President Francisco Morales Bermúdez has tried to consider some CONACO requests, though not to the extent the government of President Fernando Belaúnde did during the period 1963-1968.

CONFEDERACION DE TRABAJADORES DE LA REVOLUCION PERUANA. The CTRP, or Federation of Workers of the Peruvian Revolution, since 1969 has been sponsored by the government to counterbalance the Communist-led General Federation of Peruvian Workers (Confederación General de Trabajadores del Peru; CGTP), which has provoked strikes to further Marxist goals. The CTRP has had a smaller membership each year during the 1970s than the CGTP.

CONFEDERACION DE TRABAJADORES DEL PERU. The CTP, or Federation of Workers of Peru, is a group of labor unions affiliated with the Aprista political party, the American Popular Revolutionary Alliance (see APRA).

CONFEDERACION GENERAL DE TRABAJADORES DEL PERU. The CGTP, or General Federation of Peruvian Workers, was organized by Communists three months before the military coup d'état of 1968, in July, and by the beginning of 1975 had become the largest of Peru's three nationwide labor union federations. In 1977, the Ministry of Labor reported that the CGTP over an eight-year period had been responsible for 67 per cent of all strikes and labor-management conflicts in the republic. At its annual national meeting, or Congress, the CGTP always has speakers and representatives from the Marxist organization, the World Federation of Trade Unions (WFTU). When the WFTU changes a position on some issue in order to please the foreign ministry of the Soviet Union,

soon thereafter the CGTP adopts a similar line. Of
special concern to the Peruvian government during the
1970s was the CGTP's control of Departmental Federation of Arequipa Workers (Federación Departamental de
Trabajadores de Arequipa; FDTA). This FDTA represents all the bureaucrats and civil servants below the
non-unionized top-level administrators in municipal, provincial, and departmental governmental entities in the
Department of Arequipa (see AREQUIPA). A general strike
called by the FDTA from time to time in the 1970s im-
mobilized all activities in public life in the Department
and the city of Arequipa.

CONSEJO DEL DISTRITO. The District Council, an entity of
government equivalent to a municipal council, functions
in each capital of a District, which is a subdivision of
a Province. The Republic of Peru administratively di-
vides into 24 Departments, subdivided into Provinces,
and further subdivided into Districts.

CONSEJO PROVINCIAL. In each city serving as the capital
of a province, a Provincial Council or Consejo Provincial functions as a municipal council, under the Organic
Law of Municipalities promulgated in 1963. Municipal
councils were elected bodies from 1892 to 1923, when
President Augusto B. Leguía replaced them by decree
with appointed councils. Forty years later, President
Fernando Belaúnde restored their status as popularly-
elected councils. Although the military governments of
President Juan Velasco (1968-1975) and President Francisco Morales Bermúdez (1975-1980) suspended the civilian national Congress, these two generals and their
ruling groups allowed the provincial and district councils
within each Department to continue to carry out local-
level government.

CONSTITUTIONALIST PARTY. In the 1900s, the Constitutionalist Party was the political vehicle of Peru's soldier-
politicians. In 1915 it agreed to back José Pardo for
President of Peru as the coalition nominee of the Constitutionalist, Liberal, and Civilista parties. He won
the election and was inaugurated in August 1915, mark-
ing a change for the Constitutionalists. After a couple
of decades of pushing military leaders, the Constitutionalists had helped elect a civilian administration. During the eleven-year dictatorship of Augusto B. Leguía
(1919-1930), only three political parties functioned openly:

Leguía's own Democratic Party, reduced to a rubber stamp for the presidency; the Liberal Party until the death of its leader Augusto Durand in 1922; and the Constitutionalist. The latter became a hollow organization for military supporters of Leguía.

CONVIVENCIA. The agreement of mutual convenience known as the convivencia was a pattern of behavior between the Apristas and the military leaders during the second term of President Manuel Prado (1956-1962), to end the violence which had ensued between Aprista and military leaders from time to time prior to 1956.

CORNEJO, MARIANO H. A pioneer modern social scientist, born in 1873. He died in 1942. In 1896 he was the first Peruvian to be appointed professor of sociology at the National University of San Marcos. His writings and lectures influenced the growth of the social sciences in Peru from the 1900s to the 1930s.

CORNEJO CHAVEZ, HECTOR. The founder of the Christian Democratic Party in Peru in 1955 (see CHRISTIAN DEMOCRATIC PARTY).

CORTE SUPREME DE JUSTICIA. The Peruvian Supreme Court of Justice, which is the apex of the judicial branch of government. It consists of eleven justices selected by Congress. During the 1968-1980 suspension of the Congress, any candidate for a vacancy on the court would be considered by the Committee or Council of Presidential Advisors, an entity created by the military government of General Juan Velasco to function in place of the suspended Congress. Supreme Court Justices have life tenure and must be native-born Peruvians, at least forty years of age, with a minimum of either twenty years of legal practice or five years of experience on the bench of a lower court to be eligible for appointment. The Supreme Court has original jurisdiction in cases involving the highest officials of government, and appellate jurisdiction over litigation from all lower courts. The Supreme Court chooses its own president or Chief Justice. The Supreme Court submits to the President of the Republic the names of prospective judges for vacancies in the lower courts and the President selects the new judges from this list of nominees.

COUP D'ETAT. During the turbulent 19th century, Peru suf-

fered several military challenges to constituted authority. In modern times, two significant coups reshaped
the political system and all public life in Peru. In June
1962, military leaders intervened to nullify a presidential election, to make sure that the longtime foe of the
military, Aprista leader Víctor Raúl Haya de la Torre,
did not become president. On October 3, 1968, a coup
ousted civilian President Fernando Belaúnde, who had
been elected in a June 1963 election, for a six-year
term beginning July 28, 1963. Led by General Juan
Velasco Alvarado, the coup brought to power a military
Junta which suspended the Congress and activities by
the political parties. On August 29, 1975, General Francisco Morales Bermúdez and a majority of the military
leaders forced General Velasco to give up the presidency
in favor of General Morales. Velasco died on December 24, 1977. The 1968 coup brought some basic changes
to Peru, ranging from expropriations of large estates
and banks to several government corporations running
the basic sectors of the economy (see MORALES BER-
MUDEZ and VELASCO ALVARADO).

CROIX, TEODORO DE. Viceroy of colonial Peru under Spanish rule during 1784-1790. He is remembered for or-
dering the burning of all books condemned by the Catholic Church or by the Spanish crown.

CUZCO. Cuzco is the name of one of the Departments of
the republic of Peru, and the Department of Cuzco is
subdivided into thirteen provinces, one of which is the
Province of Cuzco. Within that province is the city of
Cuzco, capital of the Inca Empire during the pre-Hispanic period. In the 1972 Census the city of Cuzco had
90,000 population; in 1977 its estimated population was
105,500. Cuzco is a principal tourist resort for foreign
visitors to Peru, as nearby lies Machu Picchu, the ancient Inca city which remained unknown to the Spaniards
who conquered Peru in the 1530s. In 1911, Hiram Bingham
discovered it and ever since, archaeologists and other scientists and scholars, as well as tourists, have come into
Cuzco in a steady stream, and then gone on into the heights
of the Andes to the "lost city" (see MACHU PICCHU).

-D-

DECEPCIONARSE. In Peruvian political language, decepcionarse means to become disenchanted with a leader.

DELGADO, WASHINGTON. Born in Cuzco in 1927, he has
lived in Lima since 1930. One of Peru's leading writers, he is a professor of Spanish literature of the National University of San Marcos. His poems have
appeared often in the Lima daily newspaper La
Prensa. Winner of the 1953 national poetry prize
in Peru.

DEL MAR, JUAN M. Minister of Government and head of
the presidential cabinet under President Ramón Castilla
during his second term (1855-1862), Del Mar put down
a revolt in Arequipa in 1856, and then put down revolts
in the northern coastal city of Trujillo.

DEL RIO, MANUEL. Minister of the Treasury under President Ramón Castilla during his first term (1845-1851).
Del Río formulated Peru's first national budget.

DELTEC BANKING CORPORATION see ULLOA, MANUEL

DEMOCRATIC FRONT. The Frente Democrática, or Democratic Front, was a political alliance formed by Luis
A. Eguiguren, who then became its candidate for President of Peru and won the 1936 election in a field of
several small-party candidates. The Apristas then
claimed that their support had elected him and that they
would formulate policies for Eguiguren. Thereupon the
government promptly cancelled the electoral results,
denying Eguiguren the presidency, and supporting General Oscar Benavides, who had succeeded as president
the ousted dictator Luis Sánchez Cerro, assassinated on
April 30, 1933. The power elite government in 1936,
after canceling the victory of the Democratic Front candidate, ruled that Benavides should serve out the full
six-year term as President, and not just the three years
which had remained in the term of Sánchez Cerro. Thus,
despite the fact that the Democratic Front won the election in 1936, Benavides remained in office into 1939.

DEMOCRATIC PARTY. Founded in 1884 by the followers of
Nicolás de Piérola, the Democratic Party functioned until 1912.

DENEGRI, AURELIO. Leader of the Civilistas, a political
group which in 1884 supported the Democratic and the
Constitutionalist Parties in driving presidential claimant

Miguel Iglesias from Peru into political exile, thereby
preventing prolonged civil strife.

DEUSTUA, ALEJANDRO O. (1849-1945). A widely influential
writer, politician, and philosophy professor. Rector
(President) of the National University of San Marcos in
the 1920s. His many writings disparaged the Indians
and attacked the tendency, which began to grow in the
1930s under the influence of the Apristas, of rediscov-
ering the greatness of the Inca Empire. As the APRA
movement in the 1930s strove to make Peruvians appre-
ciative of their Indian heritage as well as their Spanish
heritage, Deustua sought to prove that Quechua Indians
were lazy and that their culture had kept the Hispanic
and mestizo (hybrid) Peruvians from achieving the level
of technological development found in Europe and North
America.

DIEZ CANSECO, PEDRO. A general and politician who became provisional President of Peru in 1867 after the
revolution against the liberal 1867 Constitution. Díez
Canseco supervised presidential elections, with José
Balta as the victor (see BALTA).

DUHARTE, RAYMUNDO. The President of the Sociedad Nacional de Industrias (SNI) in 1973. His opposition to
the economic reforms of the military government resulted in an executive order preventing his return to
Peru from a business trip in November 1973. In late
1975, he was given permission to return to Lima.

DURAN REY, RAFAEL. Born on October 24, 1922, in Lima.
Graduated from the Escuela Naval and commissioned in
the Navy in 1942. Promoted to rear admiral in 1971,
having graduated from the Center for Higher Military
Studies in 1967. During 1971, Admiral Durán was chief
of strategy for the Navy. In 1974 he became naval attaché at the Peruvian Embassy in Washington, where
he helped promote mutual understanding of major public
policies and problems between the United States and
Peru.

DURAND, AUGUSTO. In 1899, Augusto Durand led an abor-
tive revolutionary uprising against the election of Eduardo
López de Romaña as President of Peru. Durand was
born in 1871 in Juánuco and was noted for his dramatic
escapes from jails, of which he was a frequent occupant

because of the revolts he led.   His thesis when he graduated from San Marcos University was titled, appropri-
ately, El derecho de rebelión (The Right of Rebellion).
Durand practiced what he preached.   In 1923, Durand,
one of the founders of the Liberal Party and from time
to time an editor of the daily newspaper La Prensa,
died under mysterious circumstances while being trans-
ferred from jail to a ship on which he was to be sent
into exile.   His death caused bitter criticism of President Augusto B. Leguía.

-E-

ECHENIQUE, JOSE RUFINO.   President of Peru during 1851-
1854, he had been Vice President under President Ramón Castilla.

EDUCATION REFORM.   On March 24, 1972, Decree Law
Number 19326 was promulgated.   It is a reform docu-
ment of 383 articles dealing with education from rural
primary schools through graduate work at universities.
Various stages of the law have gone into effect each
year, with 1980 as the target date for the last provision
of this basic reform law to take effect.   The Hispanic-
oriented classical education spawned by aristocrats in a
system which until the 1940s ignored the needs of Indians
and rural mestizos has been reshaped.   Inasmuch as 40
per cent of all Peruvians have an Indian language for a
mother tongue rather than Spanish, the Education Law
provides for rural and small-town primary and secondary
schools to offer instruction in Quechua and Aymará, as
well as in Spanish.   For the first time, Peruvian women
were given equal opportunities with men to study any vo-
cational field in trade schools and in any professional
field at the universities.

EGUIGUREN, LUIS A.   In the election of October 1936, Eguiguren was the presidential candidate of the Democratic
Front, a coalition.   When he ended his close association
with Jorge Prado, Eguiguren thereby gained the support
in his campaign from the APRA.   Balloting took place
on October 11.   After two weeks of vote counting by
hand, the Electoral Commission reported that Eguiguren
apparently had a plurality sufficient for election, approximately 40 per cent of the votes.   Prado and other candidates divided the remaining 60 per cent of the votes.

Suddenly an Election Board at the presidential palace
disqualified Eguiguren on the grounds that his vote total
included many ballots cast by Apristas at a time when
the APRA technically was proscribed. President Benavides installed a cabinet of military officers, who ordered the election results nullified. Benavides's term
of office was extended for three additional years. Eguiguren, a member of Congress, urged the Chamber of
Deputies and the Senate to impeach Benavides, but instead, Congress dissolved its own sessions. Ignored
by the Benavides administration, threatened by a small
fascist group of black shirts, and ridiculed by leftist
groups, Eguiguren padlocked his Democratic Front offices.

EIELSON, JORGE EDUARDO. Born in 1921. A prominent
sculptor, painter, and novelist. He won the 1945 National Poetry Prize. His 1957 novel El cuerpo de Giuliano (The Body of Giuliano) was a success all over Latin America and Europe. He won the 1947 National
Theater Prize for his adaptations.

ENCINAS, JOSE ANTONIO. Born in 1886, died in 1958.
Prominent as Land Commissioner in 1918, he drew up
a program to help Indians regain lands which had been
stolen from them by white aristocratic lawyers. Some
of his findings were rediscovered in 1969 after the government of President Juan Velasco promulgated the Agrarian Reform Law. This degree of June 24, 1969, with
196 articles, provided for the breaking up of unworked
large estates. The section creating peasant cooperatives
reflected in part the earlier writings of Encinas.

ENTREGUISMO. The practice of surrendering power to for-
eigners. The deliverance of Peru's resources to wealthy
Peruvian or foreign individuals or corporations by government officials. "Entreguismo" is one of the most
insulting practices one Peruvian politician can accuse a
rival of engaging in.

ESCOBAR, ALBERTO. Born in 1929 in Lima. Received
doctorates in literature and in linguistics at the Universities of Madrid and Munich. Vice-Rector of the National University of San Marcos during 1969-1971. Visiting professor at Kansas, Cornell, and New Mexico State
Universities. His volume of essays, La narración en
el Perú, published in 1960, established Escobar as Peru's
leading literary critic.

ESCUELA MILITAR.   A rudimentary military academy offer-
ing a basic course for potential officers for six-month
periods was established in the 1850s at Chorrillos, then
a small town 30 kilometers south of Lima but today a
suburb adjacent to metropolitan Lima and Miraflores.
Peruvian President Nicolás de Piérola in 1896 contracted
with a French military mission to reorganize the academy
at Chorrillos into the Escuela Militar, the Peruvian
equivalent of France's St. Cyr or the United States's
West Point, to develop a modern professional officer
corps.   By World War I advanced training for higher
ranking officers at the Escuela Superior de Guerra (Army
War College) also had been established near the Escuela
Militar at Chorrillos.   In 1958, also adjacent to the
Escuela Militar in the same area of the original armory
site, the Centro de Altos Estudios Militares (Center for
Higher Military Studies) was founded, to give officers
high level instruction before promoting them to generals
and admirals.   The Escuela Militar trains teenage cadets to become second lieutenants in the army.   Students
attend academic classes mornings and engage in rugged
military duties and athletics afternoons.   On Friday afternoons, the Escuela Militar's colorful dress parade,
with cadets in fancy dress uniforms, attracts both foreign
and Peruvian tourists.

ESCUERO OYARCE, GILBERTO.   Secretary-General of the
National Association of Journalists of Peru, 1970-1972.
He fought unsuccessfully to keep the government from
enacting the restrictive Press Law of 1970, under which
newspapers were subsequently expropriated "to further
the revolution. "

ESTUDIOS ANDINOS.   The journal Estudios Andinos was published from 1971 to 1977 at the Latin American Studies
Center of the University of Pittsburgh.   A grant from
the Ford Foundation permitted the transfer of this Spanish-language scholarly journal about the social sciences
in Peru and other Andean republics to the Universidad
del Pacífico in Lima in 1977.   In the United States, it
had been edited by Edward Cleary.   In Peru, Guido
Pennano and Alejandro Lavalle became its editors.

-F-

FAJARDO, CONSTANTINO.   The jurist who modernized and

codified procedural legislation and legal forms used in
Peruvian civil litigation, with his Manual del litigante
in 1901.

FAMILY PLANNING. On September 3, 1976, the concept of
family planning was officially accepted by a Peruvian
government for the first time in the history of this Catholic republic, where church leaders have always fought
any governmental programs which could limit the birth
rate.   In the 1970s, Peru's population began increasing
by 3.2 per cent a year, as the death rate went down
and the total population rose from seven million in 1940,
to eight million in 1950, to 13 million in 1970, to 16
million in 1978.   Throughout the 1970s, each year found
Peru with net increments of potential workers far beyond
the capacity of the national economy to absorb.   Earlier
attempts of the government to recognize the problem of
over-population were stopped short by lobbyists for the
Catholic hierarchy, in 1963 and in 1969.   The National
Commission on Population, created by the government
in September 1976, was charged with planning programs
to encourage Peruvians to plan the births of their children and to have fewer children.   Dr. Napoleón Zegarra
was named president of the Commission and Dr. Luz
Jefferson, a physician with the Ministry of Health, drew
up the charter for the Population Commission.   In addition, a privately-funded and privately-directed Council
on Population in 1977 began circulating literature on
contraceptives to women visiting its library in Lince,
a Lima suburb.   Unlike the Family Planning Centers
throughout Mexico, which since 1973 have distributed
contraceptive pills to women free of charge, in Peru
in 1977 the Ministry of Health merely distributed literature on the subject.   Impoverished peasant women were
not able to purchase pills at pharmacies.

FAUCETT, ELMER.   A commercial pilot from the United
States who pioneered commercial aviation in Peru.   In
1930, Faucett piloted the airplane which brought Colonel
Luis Sánchez Cerro from Arequipa to Lima, to oust
President Augusto B. Leguía from office by a show of
military force.   Since colonial days, leaders of revolutions had gone overland by horseback, or since the 1920s
by military trucks, from Arequipa to Lima, or else had
gone by land from Arequipa to the southern port of Mollendo, and thence by ship to Callao, on Lima's doorstep.
Peru had witnessed many such land and sea thrusts from

Arequipa upon Lima. In 1930, however, Faucett dem-
onstrated that the air age had arrived in Peru militarily.

FAUCETT AIRLINE. A privately owned airline connecting the
various provincial cities of Peru with Lima. With increasing governmental control and ownership of basic
services and industries after the advent of military government since October 1968, Faucett in the 1970s had to
share its air routes with the government's own airline,
Aeroperú (see AEROPERU).

FERNANDEZ MALDONADO, JORGE. Born on May 29, 1922,
in Ilo. Graduated from the Escuela Militar and commissioned in the Army in 1943. Military attaché in
Buenos Aires during 1959-1961. Chief of Army Intelligence from October 1968 to March 1969. Promoted to
brigadier general in 1969 and to division general in 1973.
Minister of Energy and Mines in the cabinet of President Juan Velasco. Prime Minister and chief of the
cabinet under President Francisco Morales Bermúdez
from August 30, 1975 to his retirement from the government on July 16, 1976. Fernández Maldonado, during the 1975-1976 period, was an advocate of a freer
press and encouraged constructive criticism. When
General Guillermo Arbulu replaced him in 1976 as Prime
Minister, government "guidance" of the mass media in-
tensified.

FINANCE. In 19th-century Peru, the Ministry of the Treasury was concerned with collecting taxes and being able
to furnish funds sufficient for maintaining traditional,
basic governmental services, ranging from road repairs
to police protection against criminals. This concept of
public finance persisted until 1945, when, in the final
year of the first term of President Manuel Prado, governmental investments to stimulate the economy went
beyond minimal proportions. During Prado's second
term (1956-1962), governmental finances again became
slightly more visible than during the decades of Peruvian
history in which political action had been punctuated by
violence in a bipolar struggle between the "ins" and the
"outs" among the economic elite. During the one-year
caretaker military government from June 1962 through
June 1963, Peru's generals hinted at the economic reforms the younger generation of officers advocated in
1968 by creating the National Institute of Planning, the
first such governmental entity in the republic's history.

During the administration of President Fernando Belaúnde
(1963-1968), this Institute urged greater governmental
involvement in the expansion of the national economy.
Special emphasis was given to public finance through developmental loans. The old Treasury Ministry had become the Ministry of Finance and Peru had modernized
its policies.

FISHERIES REFORM LAW. Decree Law Number 18350 was
promulgated on April 14, 1970, as one of the basic institutionalized reforms of the military government of
President Juan Velasco. This law confirmed the government's control over all Peruvian marine resources
up to 200 miles from the shoreline and spelled out the
Ministry of Fisheries' authority to direct all aspects of
the fishing and fish products industries. The law also
created as government corporations the Public Fisheries
Services Company (Empresa Pública de Servicios de
Pesca; EPSEP) and the Public Fishmeal and Fishoil
Marketing Company (Empresa Pública de Comercio de
Harina de Pesca; EPCHAP). In May 1973, all public
entities relating to the production, marketing, processing,
and catching of fish and fish products were placed under
the government corporation called Pescaperú. During
1973-1975, the Ministry of Fisheries and Pescaperú
jointly governed all fishing activities in the republic.
During 1976 and 1977, President Francisco Morales
Bermúdez, in order to bolster the national economy,
which was suffering from inflation and excessive bureaucratic regulation, encouraged a moderate move away
from total public enterprise in the fishing industry, al-
lowing some participation by private companies. The
Comunidad Pesquera (Fishing Community), a cooperative
for workers, created by the military leaders during the
leftward thrust of their revolution (1968-1975), continued
to function during the moderating phase (1975-1980).

FLORIAN, MARIO. Born in 1917. Called the "social poet"
of the 1940s, Mario Florián became one of the few Peruvian writers to make the white and mestizo literary
circles of Lima aware of the oral poetic tradition of
the Indians. His works frequently interspersed Quechua
words in his Spanish-language poems, introducing various phrases from the Andean villages to coastal cities
for the first time. His Poesía escrita (Written Poetry),
published in 1961, was circulated widely in most Peruvian universities.

FLOTA MERCANTE.   The Merchant Marine of Peru consists
of both privately-owned and government-owned fleets of
merchant ships, hauling cargo to and from Peruvian
ports to foreign ports around the world.   The private
corporation Naivera Humboldt throughout the 1960s and
1970s operated the Peruvian merchant ships with the
largest tonnage in the nation's merchant marine, ranging from 26,176 dead-weight tons to 28,263 for its largest vessel, the Motonave Salcantay.

FOCEP.   The Frente Obrero, Campesino, Estudantil y Pop-
ular--or Popular, Student, Peasant and Worker Front--
was organized in late 1977 by followers of Trotskyite-
Marxist leader Hugo Blanco, who was living in exile in
Argentina in lieu of serving the remainder of a twenty-
year prison term for murdering two police officers in
1963.   FOCEP drew its major support from peasant
unions in Cuzco, university student federations in Cuzco
and other provincial areas, and the defunct Cuban-Peru-
vian Friendship Clubs.

FRESCO.   In small towns of the Andes, a fresco is a cold
drink made of sugar and fruit juice.   The word becomes
refresco or gaseoso in the larger coastal cities, especially in metropolitan or greater Lima.

-G-

GALLETA.   Literally, the word galleta means cracker or
biscuit, but in Peruvian political circles it has come to
mean a cowardly politician.

GALVEZ, JOSE (1819-1866).   A prominent educator who established and administered several school systems.   As
a politician, Gálvez was a radical liberal and fought conservative policies at the national and local levels.   An
advisor to President Ramón Castilla, Gálvez was the ad-
ministrator who insisted on some restrictions on the political activities of Catholic Church bishops.   He is remembered principally as the Minister of the Treasury
who signed and promulgated the decree ending special
tribute or taxes via extra work on the part of the Indians,
proclaimed into law in July 1854.

GALVEZ VELARDE, AUGUSTO.   A vice admiral in the Navy,
he was appointed Minister of Housing on June 5, 1974,

and during the period 1974-1975 launched many of Peru's
largest public housing projects.

GAMARRA, AGUSTIN. Born in 1788 in Lima, he was killed
on November 8, 1841, leading his troops against Bolivian
troops at the battle of Ingavi. Under General Antonio
Sucre, General Gamarra was one of the heroes at the
Battle of Ayacucho in 1824, helping expel the army of
Spain from newly-independent Peru. In June 1829, Ga-
marra deposed President José de la Mar for getting
Peru involved in war with Colombia. On August 31,
1829, Congress elected Gamarra as President of Peru.
His domineering wife, Francisca, became known as La
Mariscala (the Woman Marshall or General). She was
widely credited for making his decisions for him.

GAMBOA PIEROLA, JOSE LUIS. Born on August 1, 1911,
in Lima. Graduated from the Escuela Militar and was
commissioned in the Army in 1966, rising in the ranks
to general. Under President Juan Velasco, from January 1969 to August 1975, Gamboa Piérola held the title
of Director General of Government, functioning as an
efficiency expert in an attempt to coordinate various
levels of public administration.

GARCIA, ENRIQUE LEON. A physician, Dr. García, as
Minister of Public Health under President Guillermo
Billinghurst (1912-1915), gave Peru its first genuinely
modern health service.

GARCIA Y GARCIA, ELVIRA (1862-1951). She began the
feminist movement in Peru, demanding education and
job opportunities for women. She successfully lobbied
to have the Army appoint its first women nurses as
medical officers in 1918. In her writings she predicted
that even in a male-led society such as Peru's, women
would someday be accepted for responsible jobs in public health and public safety. Sixteen years after her
death, in 1977 Peru graduated its first women medical
paratroopers in the Army's rescue service and added
women to its traffic police to unclog downtown parking
in Lima.

GARCIA PUMACAHUA, MATEO. The Peruvian general who
commanded the first major attack for independence
against Spanish forces in August 1814 in Cuzco. His
second and third in command were the brothers José

and Vicente Angulo. They then captured Arequipa before Viceroy Abascal could concentrate troops there, but were defeated by Spanish troops in early 1815.

GARCILASO DE LA VEGA. Born in 1539, son of a Spanish conqueror and an Indian mother of the Inca nobility. The most famous mestizo (hybrid) of the colonial period, he was known as "El Inca." His book Comentarios reales became a valuable source on pre-Hispanic government and culture (see COMENTARIOS REALES and AYLLU).

GASEOSO see FRESCO

GONZALEZ PRADA, MANUEL (1848-1918). From an aristocratic Lima family, he emerged as an intellectual after the War of the Pacific defeat by Chile, to help regenerate Peru's national spirit. In 1891, he organized the Unión Nacional as a political party. After 1898, he began to preach anticlericalism and atheism, urging that Peruvians substitute science and humanism for Catholicism. In 1902, he abandoned his UN party to proclaim himself an anarchist. He became the most publicized radical in Peruvian public life.

GRACE, W. R. An Irishman who launched his career in Peru in 1850 with a British-Peruvian commercial firm. After marrying Lillian Gilchrist, daughter of an American captain of a merchant ship, Grace moved to the United States, leaving his younger brother, Michael, in charge of his Peruvian operations. In 1862, Grace established an export-import company in New York which by 1870 operated its own cargo ship between New York and Callao.

GRACE AND COMPANY. In 1871, W. R. and Michael Grace in Lima bought the company's first industrial plant in Peru, the Vitarte textile mill. By 1881, W. R. Grace and Company owned and operated large sugar plantations and Peru's first large, modern sugar refineries. In the 20th-century, the Grace company operated cargo and passenger ships between Peruvian and U.S. ports, and in the 1940s and 1950s operated jointly with Pan American Airways the Panagra Airline. In the 1960s, Grace sold its airline operations to rival Braniff Airlines. After 1968, its plantations were expropriated by the military reform government.

GRAHAM HURTADO, JOSE. Born in 1918 in Arequipa.
Graduated from the Escuela Militar and commissioned
in the Army in 1941. Graduated from the Center for
Higher Military Studies in 1959, and was promoted to
brigadier general in 1969. From October 1968 through
February 1969 he was Prefect of the Province of Lima,
which includes the national capital, the city of Lima.
On March 1, 1969, he was chosen to head the Council
of Presidential Advisors (Comité de Asesoramiento a
la Presidencia; COAP), putting him in charge of a key
entity of the military reform governments of President
Juan Velasco and then President Francisco Morales
Bermúdez during the decade 1968-1978. The COAP,
with 42 to 45 generals and admirals with top-level administrative experience, functioned in place of the suspended Congress, which was scheduled to be revived
with the 1980 elections.

GRAU, MIGUEL. A native of Piura, Miguel Grau became
an early leader of Peru's fledgling navy, first distin-
guishing himself in 1856 fighting against the government
of President Ramón Castilla. In 1872, as commander
of the warship Huáscar, Grau defeated vessels of the
rebel forces under General Tomás Gutiérrez, who had
ousted President José Balta. In the War of the Pacific
against Chile, at the battle of Iquique on May 21, 1879,
Admiral Grau saved his flagship, the Huáscar, as Chilean ships sank Peru's most modern warship, the Independencia. During the next five months, Grau became
the scourge of the Chilean navy, capturing Chilean ships
all along Chile's coast. On October 8, 1879, at the
Battle of Angamos, Grau was killed. The Merchant
Marine College at Callao, which trains cadets as officers, is named in his honor. Grau graduates command
Peru's merchant ships.

GUAMAN POMA DE AYALA, FELIPE. A Quechua Indian
schooled by Spaniards who wrote a famous chronicle,
Nueva Crónica y el Buen Gobierno, in 1611. Guamán
spent thirty years writing his book, which ranks second
only to Garcilaso de la Vega's Comentarios Reales as
the outstanding indigenous literature in Peru's Spanish
colonial era.

GUANO. Anchovy living in the cold water of the Humboldt
Current feed millions of aquatic birds, whose excre-
ment, called guano, makes excellent fertilizer. Exports

of guano from the 1840s to the 1890s made Peru an important trading nation around the globe. During this so-called Guano Era Peru's coastal region assumed a position of dominance within the republic's economy. Yet the prosperity of the coastal region, as well as that of the entire Peruvian economy, became subject in the latter half of the 19th-century to the vicissitudes of world trade. New mining enterprises and a more commercial-type of agriculture for export of cotton, plus textile mills at the turn of this century began to overshadow the fertilizer export market. In the 1860s, scientists discovered that nitrate of soda manufactured from caliche (mineral salt just below the surface of the soil of Peru) also made excellent fertilizer. Also in the 1860s, the invention of powerful explosives made from nitrates from Peru's deserts drew some attention away from exporting guano. In the 20th century, fertilizers produced from petroleum byproducts took over the fertilizer market previously enjoyed by the guano exporters.

GUEVARA, PABLO. Born in 1930 in Lima. Studied writing in Europe. Winner of the 1954 National Poetry Prize. Throughout the 1950s he was publisher of the magazine Letras Peruanas. In the 1960s and 1970s he taught motion picture writing courses in Lima, helping the budding Peruvian film industry develop its own production personnel.

GUTIERREZ, MIGUEL. Born in 1940. He was a professor of literature in Icá, Ayacucho, and then Lima. His novel Matavilela, published in 1968, shocked critics with its scatology. His 1969 novel, El viejo se retira (The Old Man Retires), is an attack on education in the provincial northern coastal city of Piura, where he was born and educated. It provoked some national discussion about educational reforms when the government was formulating the 1972 Education Reform Law.

GUTIERREZ CUEVAS, TEODOMIRO. During the presidency of Guillermo Billinghurst (1912-1915), Teodomiro Gutiérrez Cuevas was director of a Commission on Indian Affairs and a strong advocate for better working conditions for Indians working in agriculture and mining. In 1913, leaders in Congress accused him of encouraging Indians to seize rural tracts of land from absentee landlords of large estates. Neither his Commission recommendations for reforms nor the charges of his congres-

sional opponents were ever finalized. He did symbolize
an early attempt at land reform later carried out by the
military governments during 1968-1978.

-H-

HAYA DE LA TORRE, VICTOR RAUL. Born in Trujillo on
    February 22, 1895. Unmarried. Attended both the Na-
    tional University of Trujillo (1915) and the National Uni-
    versity of San Marcos (1917), but did not graduate. At
    San Marcos, he was president of the Federation of Stu-
    dents and a leader of the 1919 student-workers' strike.
    He was sent into exile by the government and in 1923
    settled for a time at the National Autonomous University
    of Mexico, not as a student but as a daily visitor with
    other political theorists. In Mexico City in 1924, Haya
    de la Torre founded what later became Peru's first truly
    disciplined and modernly organized political party, the
    APRA or Alianza Popular Revolucionaria Americana
    (American Popular Revolutionary Alliance). He served
    as the APRA presidential candidate in those elections
    in which APRA was permitted to participate: in 1931,
    1962, and 1963. As the leader of the largest political
    party in Peru, he had a profound influence on Peruvian
    political life throughout the 1960s. APRA itself began
    as pro-Communist but became anti-Communist when Haya
    realized that his social reform goals were better served
    within a framework of Peruvian nationalism than in sub-
    servience to the policies of the Soviet Union. (See
    ALIANZA POPULAR REVOLUCIONARIA AMERICANA.)
    In 1977, at age 82, Haya again offered a series of lec-
    tures in various Peruvian cities, to rally the APRA to
    organize and search for candidates for the scheduled
    1978 and 1980 elections.

HUAMACHUCO. A village in the sierra of Peru where the
    great liberator Simón Bolívar made his final military
    preparations in 1824 for the final battles to drive the
    Spaniards out of Peru, culminating in the Battle of Aya-
    cucho, in December 1824.

HUANCAVELICA. One of the twenty-four Departments into
    which the republic of Peru is divided administratively.
    The Department of Huancavélica is subdivided into five
    provinces, one of which also is named Huancavélica
    Province.

HUANCAYO. A city high in the central Andes which is the inland terminal for the Central Railroad line from Lima on the coast.

HUANUCO. One of the twenty-four Departments in which Peru is geographically divided. The Department of Huánuco is subdivided into seven Provinces, one of which is named the Province of Huánuco.

HUASCAR. The half-brother of Ataphualpa, with whom he fought a civil war in the 1520s over the inheritance of the title of emperor of the Inca Empire. When Huayna Capac, the eleventh Inca emperor, died in A.D. 1525, his son, Huáscar, claimed the throne from his palace in Cuzco. But his half-brother, Atahualpa, who had been living with their father in the other seat of empire in Quito, Ecuador, also proclaimed himself emperor. The civil war lasted until 1531, when Atahualpa defeated Huáscar, whom he then imprisoned. When Francisco Pizarro landed in northern Peru in 1532 with 180 Spanish soldiers, he learned of the hatred and division between the followers of Atahualpa and Huáscar. In November 1532, Pizarro took Atahualpa prisoner and in July 1533 executed him. While still a prisoner of the Spaniards, Atahualpa had sent orders from his cell to his followers to kill Huáscar. A Quechua, not a Spaniard, therefore, actually took Huáscar's life.

HUMBOLDT, BARON ALEXANDER VON. Born on September 14, 1769, in Berlin, he also died there on May 6, 1859. Baron von Humboldt is best remembered for his 1802-1803 explorations in Ecuador, but the famed naturalist also visited Callao and Lima, and the warm current or stream he identified in the midst of the colder Pacific waters flanking it was named in his honor. The Humboldt Current is a vital factor to Peruvian fishing fleets all along the coast of the republic.

-I-

ICA. One of the twenty-four administrative Departments into which Peru is divided geographically. The Department of Icá is subdivided into five Provinces, one of which is the Province of Icá. Within that Province lies the ancient city of Icá, fifty kilometers inland from the ocean, 220 kilometers south of Lima.

IGLESIAS, MIGUEL. General Iglesias, acting on behalf of a
    defeated Peru, signed the Treaty of Ancón which ended
    hostilities with Chile on October 23, 1883. He became
    interim President of Peru until August 1884.

INCA. The word "Inca" popularly refers to the Indians of a
    vast pre-Hispanic empire, but technically the Inca was
    the ruler of that empire, whereas his subjects princi-
    pally were Quechua and Aymará Indians. By 1200 B. C.
    the Chavín culture prevailed in the northern highlands
    of Peru. Its emphasis on feline deities and monsters
    carved out of stone suggests a preoccupation with fright-
    ening spirits and power. The Chavíns built large cities
    along the desert coast of Peru and in the highlands of
    Bolivia. Because of the extreme dryness of the climate,
    archaeologists have been able to excavate many of their
    remains almost intact. Pachacamac, in the central
    coastal region (near where the Spaniards built modern
    Lima), flourished as a cultural center. Near Lake Ti-
    ticaca was the city of Tiahuanaco. When the Spaniards
    conquered the Inca Empire in 1533, the Inca, from the
    Inca capital of Cuzco, ruled lands stretching from Quito,
    Ecuador in the north to the Chilean deserts in the south.

INDIGENISTA. Members of the Indigenous Reform Movement,
    which began in 1889 as a political action club for intel-
    lectuals. By the 1920s, Indigenismo reached its peak,
    and began being absorbed into the Aprista philosophy
    which Víctor Haya de la Torre launched in 1924.

INGAVI, BATTLE OF. At the Battle of Ingavi, on November
    18, 1841, Bolivian troops routed Peruvians and killed
    General Agustín Gamarra, who had served as President
    of Peru after being elected by Congress in 1829. Bo-
    livians invaded Peru from the south while Ecuadorian
    troops entered Peru from the north. Peruvian field
    commanders became confused in a multi-sided civil war
    which followed.

INTERNATIONAL PETROLEUM COMPANY. The subsidiary
    of Standard Oil of New Jersey, IPC became a celebrated
    cause for a crisis culminating in the ouster of President
    Fernando Belaúnde on October 3, 1968, by a military
    junta under General Juan Velasco. For months preced-
    ing that coup, Peru crackled with public debate and in-
    flamed newspaper editorials about the merits and de-
    merits of expropriating IPC. The day the government

expropriated the property and installations of IPC, October 9, 1968, has been celebrated ever since as a national holiday called "Day of National Dignity," to emphasize its emotional importance for Peruvian nationalism. The expropriation of the IPC led to the establishment of the governmental corporation Petroperú, to control all exploration, drilling, transporting, refining, and marketing of oil in Peru. Standard Oil had created IPC in 1916 to take over a British company, the London and Pacific Petroleum Company, at the La Brea and Pariñas oil fields. IPC inherited the British firm's privileged treatment and sizable tax concessions. By 1930, IPC produced 80 per cent of Peruvian oil and 90 per cent of its natural gas. In 1946, IPC got even larger, being granted government concessions in the Sechura area, which until then had been reserved for the government's own fledgling State Oil Company. In 1957, IPC took over the remaining Peruvian oil fields at Lobitos. Popular resentment increased for a decade, culminating in the 1968 expropriation.

INTIRRAIMI. The Quechuan name for the festival of the summer solstice. After the Spanish conquest and the conversion of Indians to Catholicism, this festival became St. John's Day on June 24 in the Gregorian calendar.

IQUITOS. A city in the north, located on the Amazon River, deep in the eastern jungle, not connected by any modern roads to the coastal cities to the west and south. The capital of the Department of Loreto, Iquitos is less than 200 kilometers from the Colombian border and 300 kilometers from the Ecuadorian border, but not connected to either by roads. Until the air age, Peruvians could get to Iquitos most easily by entering the Amazon River on the Atlantic Ocean at Belém and sailing up the mighty river through northern Brazil for 3,000 kilometers, crossing a tiny portion of Colombia wedged between Brazil and Peru at the town of Leticia, and westward on the Amazon River inside northeasternmost Peru to Iquitos. This slow voyage took two weeks by sailing ship and one week by steamship. Today jet airplanes take passengers from Lima to Iquitos in one hour.

-J-

JAGUAY. An Indian folk song, popularly sung by field hands during any harvest.

JAUREGUI, AGUSTIN. Viceroy of Peru during 1781-1784, he had to make peace between arch-conservatives fighting courses in modern science at the National University of San Marcos and assertive liberals demanding that some science lectures be given, even if opposed by the Catholic hierarchy. The viceroy did allow liberal aristocrats to maintain Masonic lodges despite protests from the Archbishop of Lima that some colonial officials were practicing freemasonry.

JIMENEZ, GUSTAVO. A general who served as Minister of War in 1931, and used troops and police to insure that there would be no violence during the election to choose a president in 1931. A new electoral law had removed property qualifications, awarding suffrage to all literate males twenty-one years of age or older. Jiménez enforced constitutional regulations in the October 1931 balloting, in which Luis Sánchez Cerro defeated Víctor Raúl Haya de la Torre for the presidency of Peru.

JUNIN. One of the twenty-four Departments into which Peru is divided administratively. The Department of Junín is subdivided into seven Provinces, one of which is the Province of Junín.

JUNIN, BATTLE OF. On the plains of Junín, General Simón Bolívar and General Antonio de Sucre combined their armies to engage the troops of Spain on August 6, 1824. In a bitter cavalry engagement of thousands of Spanish and Peruvian troops in a battle which lasted only forty-five minutes, the fate of Peru's struggle for independence was largely decided. Spanish ranks were decimated by triumphant Peruvians. Only one more battle lay ahead, that of Ayacucho on December 9, after which Peru's independence from Spain became permanent.

-K-

K. This letter is not in the Spanish alphabet but is employed in some transliterations or transcriptions of Quechua (Kechua) and in foreign words and proper names. Usually words beginning with "K" can be found under the letter "Q."

KELLOGG, FRANK. United States Secretary of State Kellogg in 1929 helped Peru and Chile settle their long-standing

feud over their border, which had been moved northward
by Chile in the War of the Pacific. He got an agreement whereby Tacna would be returned to Peru and Arica
would remain in Chile.

-L-

LA BREA FIELDS. The La Brea and Pariñas oilfields, near
the northern coastal settlement of Talara, were bought
by the London and Pacific Petroleum Company in 1889.
In 1916, Standard Oil of New Jersey negotiated to ac-
quire them and in 1924 turned them over to its subsidiary, International Petroleum Company, for development.
In October 1968, these fields were expropriated by the
government, along with all other facilities of the IPC.

LAFTA. The acronym for Latin American Free Trade Association, established in 1960 to promote a Latin American common market. Peru is a member of both LAFTA
and the smaller regional Andean Pact agreement. Ten
South American republics plus Mexico are members of
LAFTA, which has its headquarters in Montevideo, Uruguay.

LA FUENTE, ANTONIO. An army colonel, he became a
general in 1823 at the age of twenty-five, defending
José de la Riva, who claimed to be acting President
of Peru, though neither Spain nor liberator Simón Bolívar recognized that claim.

LA LIBERTAD. One of the twenty-four administrative De-
partments into which Peru is divided geographically.
The Department of La Libertad is subdivided into seven
Provinces.

LAMBAYEQUE. One of the twenty-four administrative Departments into which Peru is divided geographically.
The Department of Lambayeque is subdivided into three
Provinces, including one named the Province of Lambayeque.

LANDAZURI RICKETTS, JUAN. Born in Arequipa in 1913.
Educated at the Universidad de San Augustín in Arequipa,
subsequently entering the priesthood. He became Archbishop of Lima in 1955, and was made a Cardinal in
1962. His sister married a former Prime Minister and

former Minister of War, General Ernesto Montagne. In June 1958, Archbishop Landázuri became enmeshed in a controversy over the disputed annulment of the 43-year-old marriage of the President. Instead of processing the annulment through the Sacred Rota in Rome, as Vatican rules prescribe, the Prado annulment was made final by a local committee of bishops in Lima. Immediately thereafter, Prado, then 69 years of age, remarried a 36-year-old woman and his wife of 43 years went into retirement in Paris. Groups of women picketed the offices of Archbishop Landázuri because the Prado annulment had claimed that neither party was aware of the marriage vows, even though the marriage was consummated with children and grandchildren. During 1963-1968, Landázuri gave moral support to the reforms of President Fernando Belaúnde. And after the military came to power in 1968, he again gave public approval for the basic changes which engendered political controversy.

LA OROYA.   A settlement in the heartland of the richest copper and other ore deposits in central Peru. La Oroya is a freight-switching depot for trains connecting the Andes to the coast at Lima and Callao.

LAVALLE, HERNANDO DE.   An unsuccessful presidential candidate in the election of 1956. Winner Manuel Prado received 568,000 votes as the National Coalition Party candidate; runner-up Fernando Belaúnde of the Popular Action received 458,000, and Lavalle got 222,000 votes. Lavalle was the candidate of independents, dissidents from the Prado group, and small minor parties which could not themselves field a candidate.

LEGUIA, AUGUSTO B.   Born in Lambayeque in 1863. Died in Lima on February 6, 1932, in prison, after an operation. Leguía completed his early education in Valparaíso, Chile, having been sent there for the mild climate. He suffered from bronchial ailments. Short and very thin, Leguía had tremendous energy, which he applied to business and politics. He became fluent in English and was therefore able to negotiate in foreign trade on his own. He became general manager of the Peruvian and Bolivian and Ecuadorian branches of the New York Life Insurance Company. He exported hides to the United States and sugar to Chile. He also was manager of the British Sugar Company of Peru. He established

his own insurance company, Compañía de Seguros Sud
América, and became president of the National Bank of
Peru.   He established the Guano Administrative Company
to market fertilizer.   During his longtime dictatorship
from 1919 to 1930, Leguía as President of Peru promulgated the Constitution of 1920 but interpreted constitutional law so as to govern in an autocratic manner.   His
eleven-year rule is known in Spanish as the onceno
(eleventh).   He made a token gesture towards decen-
tralized power by creating three regional legislatures
to deal with non-vital provincial matters.   Leguía spoke
vaguely of social benefits, and multiplied the national
debt tenfold by printing bonds for New York bankers to
sell to trusting investors in the United States.   After
the economic depression in 1929 in the United States
dried up investments, Leguía lost the source of the funds
which had enabled him to continue bribing his trusted
army and police officers.   In 1930, Leguía was ousted
from the government, sent to prison, and when he died
there after an operation, weighed only 67 pounds, almost a skeleton of his former normal 140 pounds.

LIBERAL PARTY.   In 1902 Augusto Durand and a group of
young men organized the Liberal Party, after almost
rejecting the name because it suggested anticlericalism.
The party took little part in the presidential election of
1903, supporting a weak candidate against the victorious
Manuel Candamo, candidate of the Constitutionalist Party
and the Civilista Party.   With the death in 1923 of Augusto Durand, its founder, the Liberal Party fell apart.

LIMA.   The capital of the republic of Peru.   Founded by the
Spanish conquerors on January 6, 1535, the day of Epi-
phany, Lima hence acquired the title, "City of Kings."
Francisco Pizarro needed a headquarters on the coast with
a natural harbor for Spanish ships linking him to the mother
country.   He rejected the idea of converting the Inca capital
of Cuzco, high in the Andes, as the viceregal capital, even
though Hernán Cortés had chosen the Aztec capital of Ten-
ochtitlán as the base for Mexico City.   By contrast, Pizarro's Lima remained a European settlement, not an amalga-
mation of Indian and Spanish cities.   The name Lima came
from corruption of the Indian word Rímac, which is the
city's river.   Although Lima's greater metropolitan population in 1977 was estimated at 3.5 million, the population within its municipal limits was considerably smaller.
That estimate included the inhabitants of the port of

Callao, and of the suburbs of Lince, Miraflores, and Chorrillos. In the 1972 Census, Lima proper counted 1,633,000 residents.

LIMA, DEPARTMENT OF. Lima is also the name of one of the twenty-four administrative Departments into which Peru is divided geographically. The Department of Lima contains seven Provinces, one of which also bears the name, Province of Lima.

LISSON, CARLOS (1823-1891). A dean of the Faculty of Letters of the National University of San Marcos who introduced the study of modern social sciences into Peruvian universities.

LLAMA. An animal indigenous to the Andes, found in the mountains of Peru, Bolivia, and to a very limited extent in Ecuador and northernmost Argentina's high peaks. This woolly-haired animal measures four feet tall at the shoulder and averages four to five feet in length. Llamas are used as pack animals, carrying up to 75 pounds, by the Indians in Andean villages. They are also household pets for millions of Quechua and Aymará families. Their sheared wool is a basic material for caps, sweaters, blouses, and coats woven by Indians for personal use and for sale to foreign and Peruvian tourists.

LONDON AND PACIFIC PETROLEUM COMPANY. This British firm in 1889 bought the La Brea and Pariñas oil fields in the northern coastal area and sold them in 1916 to Standard Oil of New Jersey, which in 1924 created the International Petroleum Company subsidiary to develop oil wells and production.

LOPEZ CAUSILLAS, ALBERTO. A lieutenant general in the Peruvian Air Force who became Minister of Air in the cabinet of President Juan Velasco from late 1968 to August 1975.

LOPEZ DE ROMAÑA, EDUARDO. In 1899, he had the backing of the Democrats and the Civilistas and won the presidency of Peru. López had served as Minister of Development after that cabinet post had been created by President Piérola. Trained as an engineer, López began to reorganize the nation's school system in 1901 to emphasize more technology in higher education. By the time of the 1903 election, López had lost his coalition backing from Democrats loyal to Piérola.

LORET DE MOLA, CARLOS.   An engineer who served as
President of Empresa Petrolera Fiscal (Fiscal Petroleum
Enterprise) before the government reorganized Petroperú
in 1971.

LORETO.   One of the twenty-four administrative Departments
into which Peru is divided geographically.   The Department of Loreto is subdivided into six Provinces, one of
which bears the name Province of Loreto, which contains the city of Iquitos, the only modern city in the
vast Amazon River-area jungle.

LORTON.   In 1917 the Peruvian ship Lorton was sunk off the
coast of Spain, and Germany refused to satisfy the Peruvian government's demands for reparations.   Peru thereupon broke diplomatic relations with Germany.

LUNA PIZARRO, FRANCISCO.   Born in Arequipa in 1780.
A priest whose mother was related to conqueror Francisco Pizarro, Luna Pizarro became attuned to the democracy emerging in the United States.   In 1822 he organized Peruvians against any continuance of monarchy
and for the establishment of a republic through the Sociedad Patriótica.

-M-

MACANA.   A shawl, also known in Spanish as a rebozo,
worn by women in northern Peru.

MACHO.   A macho is a virile male.   Machismo is the life-
style of demonstrating masculinity by dominating women
and by displaying physical courage when challenged.   It
also means showing virility by impregnating one's wife
or girl friends as often as nature allows and gives rise
to widespread Peruvian male reluctance to practice birth
control.   In politics, machismo means defeating all op-
posing candidates and defeating their programs and pro-
posals, a concept which has made European and North
American-style political compromise difficult to achieve
in Peru.

MACHU PICCHU.   A city of the Incas hidden from the Spaniards in the jungle vegetation seventy kilometers north-
west of Cuzco, Machu Picchu served as a hideout for
Manco Inca after his unsuccessful rebellion against the

Spanish conquerors in 1535-1556. Finally, in 1911,
Professor Hiram Bingham of Yale University discovered
the lost city of Machu Picchu, which urban Peruvian and
foreign historians and archaeologists had heard about in
assumed legends and folktales for centuries. By the
1970s, anthropologists had pieced together enough sketchy
clues to conclude that Machu Picchu functioned as a se-
cret court for Inca nobility who had fled Spanish rule
from the 1530s through the 1560s. A solid fortress and
series of residences and temples, Machu Picchu became
an attraction to American and other tourists in the 1950s,
when daily railroad service from Cuzco traversed the
tortuous terrain of the Andean peaks engulfing the hidden
ancient city.

MADRE DE DIOS.   One of the twenty-four administrative Departments into which Peru is divided geographically.
The Department of Madre de Díos is subdivided into
three provinces.   It is located in easternmost central
Peru, along the Brazilian border.

MAGDALENA.   A town on the edge of Lima which has grown
in population and territory in the 1970s and is now considered a Lima suburb.

MANAVALE.   Among northern coastal villagers, anyone called
manavale is useless or inept.   A term of marked insult
in political debates and campaigns.

MANZANILLA, JOSE M.   A pioneer professor of economics
in the modern social-science sense, who in 1895 began
teaching at the National University of San Marcos.   He
took the old course in economic history and converted
it into quantitative courses in economic policy and economic legislation, the latter somewhat akin to modern
courses in policy formulation.

MARAÑON RIVER.   The Marañón River in northeastern Peru
converges with the Ucayali River south of Iquitos, at a
juncture where both these rivers merge into the Amazon
River.

MARCO DEL PONT, GUILLERMO.   He graduated from the
Escuela Militar and was commissioned in the Army in
1944.   Promoted to brigadier general in 1970 and to division general in 1974.   He was director of the government's National Planning Institute for several years.

Appointed Minister of Economy and Finance on January 8, 1974. In July 1974, he retired in poor health. His elaborate planning studies have been utilized throughout the 1970s by subsequent high-level planning administrators.

MARIATEGUI, JOSE CARLOS (1895-1930). A Marxist journalist-essayist frequently cited as the godfather of theoretical socialism in Peru. In 1926 Mariátegui declared that he was an Indigenista (a member of the Indigenous Reform Movement) because he was a socialist, and that socialism and indigenism in Peru should merge. Before the era of Víctor Raúl Haya de la Torre and APRA, Mariátegui was Peru's most prominent revolutionary political theorist. His fame rested in part on the volume, Seven Interpretive Essays on Peruvian Reality.

MARQUEZ, MELGAR. On March 6, 1932, an eighteen-year-old Aprista named Melgar Márquez tried to assassinate the President of Peru, Luis Sánchez Cerro in the Church of Miraflores and succeeded in critically wounding him. Sánchez Cerro recovered and served as Chief Executive until succeeded by Oscar R. Benavides in 1933.

MARTIN DE PORRAS, (1579-1639). Saint Martín de Porras, a mulatto of Indian and African origins, came from a very poor family. He became a priest and devoted himself to caring for the poor. After his canonization he became the patron saint of Peru's lowest classes. In the late 16th and early 17th centuries, four outstanding Catholics so distinguished themselves that they achieved sainthood. In addition to San Martín de Porras, they were Santa Rosa of Lima, the patron saint of Peru; Toribio Mogrovejo, outstanding Archbishop of Lima; and Francisco Solano, said to have been able to calm wild beasts and warring Indians by playing his violin.

MARTINEZ DE LA TORRE, RICARDO. In 1928 Martínez de la Torre helped José Carlos Mariátegui found the Peruvian Socialist Party. Also helping was Eudocio Ravines, who years later became an anti-Marxist and vigorous anti-Communist writer. On orders from the Communist International from Moscow to the party leaders in Lima, this party took the name Peruvian Communist Party (Partido Comunista Peruano; PCP) in 1930. Since 1964, the PCP has been divided into pro-Soviet Union and pro-China rival groups. Martínez has become one of the PCP founders annually venerated in party speeches.

MAYER DE ZULEN, MORA (1868-1959). A distinguished
    writer who held status among Peruvian intellectuals in
    an age before women could easily be accepted as social
    commentators. Her many essays and articles championed
    social reforms for Indians. She was one of the few wri-
    ters on economics in the popular sphere who warned
    throughout the 1920s that President Augusto B. Leguía's
    apparent prosperity was suspect because it was not based
    on improved production and work habits, nor on internal
    capitalization.

MEDITACIONES SOBRE EL DESTINO. Historian Jorge Basadre
    in 1939 published his Meditaciones sobre el destino his-
    tórico del Perú, widely acknowledged as a masterpiece
    of Peruvian literature. It indicated faith in the ultimate
    ability of Peru to surmount its many problems in public
    life. Basadre is the scholar who also wrote the multi-
    volume Historia de la república del Perú, published from
    1949 through 1956.

MEIGGS, HENRY. Born on July 7, 1811, in Catskill, New
    York. Died on September 29, 1877, in Lima. Ran a
    transportation service for gold miners in California in
    1849. Then he built bridges and a railroad line in
    Chile, linking Santiago with Valparaiso in 1863. Moved
    to Peru in 1868. President of Peru José Balta had
    Meiggs enter a partnership with the government in a
    mixed public-private corporation. Meiggs constructed
    two railroads, the first connecting the southern port of
    Mollendo with Arequipa, Peru's second largest city, and
    extending to the city of Puno at Lake Titicaca and on to
    Juliaca. This line ultimately extended to the city of
    Cuzco, the old Inca capital. The second railroad ran
    from Callao, the port city adjacent to Lima, to the min-
    ing region of Huancayo, high in the Andean Mountains.
    This line, the highest railroad in the world, zooming
    from sea-level to trestles 18,000 thousand feet above
    sea-level, opened the interior of Peru to large-scale
    copper and silver mining exports. Meiggs's railroad
    building brought large numbers of Chinese immigrants
    into Peru to work in laying the tracks. Today their
    descendants represent hundreds of thousands of hybrid
    Chinese-Indian-Spanish-type Peruvians. When President
    Balta died in 1872, Peru's economy became unstable,
    and the vast fortune Meiggs earned building railroads
    in Chile, Costa Rica (while he was completing his Peru-
    vian lines), and Peru disappeared along with Peru's pros-
    perity, which Meiggs had helped to generate.

MENESES, RAUL. Born on June 19, 1926, in Arequipa.
Graduated from the Escuela Militar and commissioned
in the Army's corps of engineers in 1948. Promoted
to brigadier general in 1973. Studied at the U.S. Command and General Staff School at Ft. Leavenworth, Kansas. For four years served President Juan Velasco as
a member of the Council of Presidential Advisors (see
MILITARY GOVERNMENT). During 1973-1975 he served
as Minister of Transportation and Communications.

MERCADO JARRIN, EDGARDO. Born on September 19, 1919,
in Barranco. Graduated from the Escuela Militar and
was commissioned in the Army in 1940. Studied at the
U.S. Command and General Staff School at Ft. Leavenworth, Kansas in 1956-57, and at the Inter-American
Defense College in Washington, D.C. in 1964. Promoted
to division general in 1970. Director of Army Intelligence during 1966-1967. In October 1968, appointed
Minister of Foreign Relations until January 3, 1972,
when he became Chief of Staff of the Army. On February 1, 1973, he became Prime Minister of the presidential cabinet, Minister of Defense, and Commanding
General of the Army. When General Francisco Morales
Bermúdez replaced General Juan Velasco as President
of Peru on August 29, 1975, General Mercado Jarrín
lost much of his central leverage as a policy formulator.

MESA. The word "mesa" in ordinary usage means "table"
within the context of furniture, or "plain" or "plateau"
within the context of geology. But politically, it is a
popular term in Peru for "polling place" in elections.

MESTIZO. A hybrid Peruvian of Indian and Spanish ethnic
origins. The word "cholo" is often interchanged with
"mestizo." When both terms are used together, "mestizo" connotes racial and "cholo" cultural admixtures of
European and Indian roots.

MILITARY GOVERNMENT. In the 19th century, after independence from Spain, Peru had many military leaders.
In fact, a majority of its earlier presidents and cabinet
ministers came from the ranks of generals. Civilian
leaders became a rarity in public life. In the 20th century, the reverse became true, with civilians gradually
outnumbering military leaders. As economic crises
grew, however, the generals again thrust themselves
into power. General Manuel Odría in November 1948

told the nation, as had Church leaders in an earlier
time, that the military leaders had become the "moral
guardians of the nation." In 1956, civilian government
returned with the six-year term of Manuel Prado. When
a three-way tie for the presidency occurred in the June
1962 election, the military again took power, for a stated
one-year period; and they kept that promise by holding
elections with the same candidates in June 1963. General Ricardo Pérez Godoy, then General Nicolás Lindley, served as interim Presidents during that caretaker
year. They created an Institute of Planning, a National
Housing Board, and a Housing Bank, building the foundation for the subsequent reforms to come under civilian
President Fernando Belaúnde during 1963-1968, under
military President Juan Velasco during 1968-1975, and
under military President Francisco Morales Bermúdez
during 1975-1980. One distinctive feature of the military administrations of 1968-1980 was a Council of Presidential Advisors (Comite de Asesoramiento a la Presidencia; COAP). The acronym COAP became as well
known as the word "Congress," the national legislature
which COAP replaced during the 1968-1980 period.

MIRAFLORES. An upper-income community south of Lima
and part of the greater Metropolitan Lima area. Miraflores contains the most expensive shops and stores in
Peru and the homes of aristocrats and high-level domes-
tic and foreign industrialists, as well as the residences
of many foreign diplomats.

MIRAFLORES, BATTLE OF. In 1881, the Battle of Miraflores near Lima found the Chilean army defeating the
Peruvian forces under Nicolás de Piérola.

MIRO QUESADA, LUIS. Born on December 5, 1880, in Lima.
Son of the founder of the daily newspaper El Comercio,
for many decades Peru's leading newspaper. Graduated
in law from the National University of San Marcos in
1905. Served as a Deputy in Congress during 1906-1912.
Mayor of Lima, 1916-1918. Dean of the Faculty of Letters of San Marcos during 1925-1926. Minister of Foreign Relations in 1931-1932. When his father was killed
in 1935, he became publisher of El Comercio. Editorially he vigorously opposed Víctor Raúl Haya de la Torre
and his party APRA (an Aprista having assassinated his
father). In 1968, he editorialized for the nationalization
of the International Petroleum Company. After the 1968

coup which established a military government, El Comercio increasingly opposed President Juan Velasco's policies. On July 26, 1974, El Comercio was taken over by the government. Miró Quesada lived out his retirement in Lima in seclusion. His son, Alejandro Miró Quesada, represented the newspaper-in-exile as a member of the Executive Committee of the Inter-American Press Association (Sociedad Interamericana de Prensa; SIP), headquartered in Miami, Florida. At the annual conference of the IAPA in October 1977 he was re-elected by the membership to the Executive Committee to serve until 1980. The IAPA did not recognize the Peruvian government's 1974 expropriation of the newspaper.

MISION ANDINA. International socio-economic development agency created by the International Labor Organization, itself a subdivision of the United Nations headquartered in Geneva. The treaty creating the Andean Mission was signed by Peru, Ecuador, and Bolivia, and the ILO in 1951.

MOLLENDO. The port city in southern Peru, 107 kilometers south by southwest of the city of Arequipa, and 347 kilometers north of the Chilean border via the Pan American Highway. Mollendo has long served as the Pacific port for the cities of Arequipa, Puno, and Moquegua.

MONTAGNE SANCHEZ, ERNESTO. Born on August 18, 1916, the son of General Ernesto Montagne, a former Prime Minister (1937-1939). Married to Isabel Landázuri Ricketts, sister of the Archbishop of Lima and the Cardinal of Peru. Graduated from the Escuela Militar and was commissioned in the Army in 1938. Promoted to brigadier general in 1963 and to division general in 1968. Retired from the Army in 1973. He studied at the U.S. Command and General Staff School at Ft. Leavenworth, Kansas, in 1950-51, and graduated from the Center for Higher Military Studies (CAEM) in Chorrillos, Peru, in 1960. He was Prefect of the Province of Lima during the 1962-63 military government. From October 3, 1964 to July 31, 1965, he was Minister of Public Education. He then became commandant of the War College (Escuela Superior de Guerra, not to be confused with CAEM--see CAEM) until January 1, 1967. Then he served as Deputy Chief of Staff of the Army, and later as Inspector General of the Army. After the October 3, 1968 coup, he became Prime Minister, Minis-

ter of Defense, and Commanding General of the Army,
as well as President of the Armed Forces Joint Command until 1969.

MONTERO, LIZARDO. An admiral in the Peruvian Navy who
had run unsuccessfully for President of Peru in 1876
against Mariano Prado. In the War of the Pacific, Admiral Montero commanded the sea and land forces which
were defeated at Tacna on May 6, 1880 by Chilean soldiers and sailors.

MONTERO ROJAS, EDUARDO. Born on November 2, 1918,
at Yurimaguas. Studied at the Royal Military Academy
at Caserta, Italy. Commissioned in the Peruvian Air
Force in 1942. Promoted to major general in 1963 and
to lieutenant general in 1970. Flight training as a pilot
at the U.S. Naval Air Base at Corpus Christi, Texas
in 1942, and at the U.S. Air Force Base at Maxwell,
Alabama in 1952. Superintendent of the Peruvian Air
Force Academy during 1963-1965. Director General
of Meteorology, 1967. Minister of Public Health and
Social Welfare in the cabinet of President Juan Velasco
from October 3, 1968 until January 1, 1970. Chief of
the Joint Command of the Armed Forces during 1970-
1976.

MORALES BERMUDEZ, FRANCISCO. Born in 1921 in Lima.
Married Rosa Pedraglio. Graduated from the Escuela
Militar and commissioned in the Army corps of engineers
in January 1943. Graduated from the Escuela Superior
de Guerra. Graduated from the Center for Higher Military Studies (CAEM) in 1967. At CAEM he wrote an
honors thesis of 24 pages on "Political Democracy" for
a course on theory of government, the theme of which
stressed the need of Peruvian leaders periodically to
relinquish power to new leaders. He served as Minister of Finance and Economy from March 19 to May 31,
1968, in the cabinet of President Fernando Belaúnde,
while on leave from the Army. He then became Director of Logistics for the Army General Staff. He was
promoted to brigadier general in 1968 and to division
general in 1972. He again served as Minister of Finance
and Commerce in the cabinet of President Juan Velasco
from February 1, 1969 to January 1, 1974, when he was
appointed commanding general of the Army. Widely re-
spected for his economic expertise, Morales Bermúdez
remained outside the "inner circle" of advisors to Pres-

ident Velasco because they were from middle-class families from provincial cities, whereas he was a Lima
aristocrat whose paternal family, Morales Bermúdez,
traced itself back to the Spanish conquerors.   His mother's family, Cerruti, likewise was of aristocratic Span-
ish-Italian lineage.   He did, however, design the agrarian reform program for the Velasco government, thereby
projecting an image as a genuine reformer, though more
conservative fiscally than Velasco.   On August 29, 1975,
responding to the urging of a majority of the Council of
Presidential Advisors (COAP), Morales Bermúdez became President of Peru, after the COAP forced Velasco
to resign.   In 1977, Morales decreed that elections would
be held in 1978 and 1980 for a civilian constituent assembly and the subsequent civilian government, the only
stipulation being that the social reforms of 1968-1980
not be cancelled after the military relinquished political
power.

MOYA.   A Quechua word used by all Indians in Peru, whether
they speak Quechua, Aymara, or any of the jungle dia-
lects.   "Moya" means a level area or a meadow in the
coastal region.   It means a garden or orchard in the
Andean villages.   And in the eastern jungle, moya de-
notes any gentle slope with enough vegetation to graze
cattle, sheep, or other livestock.

MUÑECAS, ILDEFONSO.   A priest who became a military
leader, Ildefonso Muñecas led Peruvians rebelling a-
gainst Spanish authority in 1812 into Bolivia (then known
as Upper Peru) and took over La Paz for several weeks
before being chased out by Spanish troops.

-N-

ÑAÑA.   A Quechua word meaning "sister."   When used by
Spanish-speaking Peruvian peasants, it has come to
mean a friend of a woman as close to her as an actual
sister.

ÑAÑO.   A Quechua word meaning "brother."   When used by
Spanish-speaking Peruvian peasants, it has come to
mean a friend of a man as close to him as an actual
brother.

NATIONAL AGRARIAN PARTY.   In 1936, the publisher of the

daily newspaper La Prensa, Pedro Beltrán, founded the
National Agrarian Party (Partido Nacional Agrario) to
promote private enterprise among farms and ranchers.
After a few years, it became inactive.

NATIONAL AGRICULTURAL UNIVERSITY. In 1921 the National Agricultural School was installed in a new campus
on the outskirts of Lima, on the former private estate
called La Molina, purchased by the government. As
agricultural experimental laboratories were added, the
school became upgraded into a university and by the
1970s had become one of the best agricultural institutions of higher learning in South America, graduating
agronomists and specialists in animal science. The Universidad Nacional de Agricultura operates model sheep
and cattle breeding farms in Puno and other provincial
cities, and model farms for scientific cultivation of rice
in the Departments of Ancash, Cajamarca, and Junín.

NATIONAL COALITION PARTY. In 1956, a hastily-formed
National Coalition Party announced that Manuel Prado
was its candidate for president. The former President
of Peru (1939-1945) had dealt gently with the Apristas
and he won their support and the election, serving a
second term during 1956-1962.

NATIONAL DEMOCRATIC FRONT. In 1945 the National Democratic Front emerged as a new political force to try to
end government by the Peruvian élite's upper-class inner
circles. In June 1945, the Front's candidate, José Luis
Bustamante, defeated rival candidate General Eloy Ureta.
President Bustamante was ousted from office on October
29, 1948, by a military junta under General Manuel
Odría.

NATIONAL DEMOCRATIC PARTY. In February 1915, José
de la Riva Agüero founded the National Democratic
Party from among an intellectual élite of professors,
writers, physicians, lawyers, and philosophers. The
newspaper La Prensa labeled the National Democrats
the "Futurists" because their ideology had been influenced by the Uruguayan philosopher José Enrique Rodó
(1872-1917), whose book Ariel (published in 1900) stressed
the need to place spiritual values above materialistic
values in public life. Soon the party of Futurists was
also known as the Arielistas. They campaigned to have
intellectuals rule Peru as a benevolent elite. The party

remained a minor but colorful group in public life for several years.

NATIONAL FRONT. A party founded to advance the presidential candidacy of Jorge Prado in 1936, but the electoral results were cancelled after Luis Eguiguren led other candidates with a plurality. Instead, Luis Sánchez Cerro's unexpired term of six years, which would have run from 1931 to 1937 had he not been assassinated in 1933, was being filled during 1933-1936 by Oscar R. Benavides. He proclaimed that he would nullify the 1936 election results and serve the full six years from the time of his own inauguration, from 1933 into 1939, and did so.

NATIONAL FRONT OF DEMOCRATIC YOUTH. In 1956, a group advocating the assimilation of Indians into mainstream Peruvian society and basic social and economic reforms. This group backed the candidacy of Fernando Belaúnde, aspirant for the presidency of the Popular Action party. Belaúnde lost in 1956 but did win the presidency in the 1963 election and served from July 28, 1963 to October 3, 1968, when a military junta ousted him.

NATIONAL PARTY. The Partido Nacional was formed by supporters of Manuel Vicente Villarán to run for the presidency in 1936, in elections which were nullified after no candidate among several won a clear majority (Luis Eguiguren led the field with a slim plurality).

NAVARRO ROMERO, ALFONSO. Contraalmirante (Rear Admiral) in the Peruvian Navy (Armada del Perú; AP). Various administrative posts in the Ministry of the Navy (Ministerio de la Marina). Minister of Culture and Justice in the cabinet of President Juan Velasco from October 1968 to late 1973.

NIETO, DOMINGO. Born in 1803 in Ilo. A military commander in Arequipa in 1834, he opposed the coup d'état which prevented the constitutionally-elected Luis José de Orbegoso from assuming the presidency. For his eloquent public pleas to observe legal institutions instead of military force, Nieto was known as the "Quijote of the Law." On April 5, 1834, at the Battle of Cangallo, Nieto's constitutionalist forces were defeated by the militarist troops led by General Miguel San Román. Later,

many of the San Román troops deserted to Nieto and
Orbegoso was able to resume the presidency.

NINACURO.   A Quechuan word meaning firefly.   Among Indians in villages high in the Andes, the word connotes
the magic of nature after sunset.

NORIEGA, ZENON.   A general who commanded the army
troops in the Lima area and suppressed the uprising by
Apristas on October 3, 1948.   A follower of General
Manuel Odría, who established a dictatorship later in
1948.

NUEVA CRONICA Y EL BUEN GOBIERNO.   A chronicle by
Felipe Huamán Poma de Ayala, written in 1611, two
years after Garcilaso de la Vega ("El Inca") published
in Spain his first volume of the Comentarios reales (see
the entry under the heading "Comentarios Reales").
Huamán Poma de Ayala, an Indian, spent thirty years
writing his Nueva crónica, which ranks second to Garcilaso's work among the outstanding indigenous literature
of colonial Peru.

NUÑEZ, ESTUARDO.   Born in 1908 in Lima.   Educated in the
German School of Lima.   Received his doctorate in literature from the National University of San Marcos in
1932.   Has been professor of literature there since 1946.
Editor of the magazine Fénix for several years, Núñez
was also Director of the National Library of Peru during 1969-1973.   In 1974-1975 he was President of the
Latin American Association of Germanic Studies.   His
book La literature peruana en el siglo XX is a standard
reference.

-O-

OBRAJES.   Work centers in Andean villages where Indians
are hired to weave wool into cloth.   The wool comes
from the Andean animals indigenous to the area, llamas
and alpacas.

ODRIA, MANUEL A.   Born in 1897 in the central Andean
town of Tarma.   Graduated from the Escuela Militar
at Chorrillos.   Promoted to brigadier general in 1946.
Minister of the Interior in the cabinet of President José
Bustamante, 1947-1948.   On October 29, 1948, he seized

the government and ousted President Bustamante, whose
administration had become chaotic. Cooperation between
the conservatives and the Apristas had ended and Senators and Deputies stayed away from sessions of Congress,
preventing a quorum. No appropriation measures could
be enacted. Odría mounted revolutionary forces in Arequipa and marched into Lima, with a junta which proclaimed him provisional President of Peru. The general
ruled for eleven years, into 1956. He outlawed the
Apristas, forcing APRA head Víctor Raúl Haya de la
Torre into sanctuary in the Colombian Embassy in Lima.
After years of legal disputes, the Peruvian government
permitted Haya safe conduct via airplane from Lima to
Bogotá.   Haya remained in exile until Odría had left office. With the coming of the Korean War (1950-1953),
the prices of Peruvian exports rose sharply and foreign
investments expanded the Peruvian economy.   Odría
agreed to end his dictatorship with an honest election
in 1956, and former President Manuel Prado was returned to power. The retired general then became a
civilian politician, forming the National Odriísta Union
(Unión Nacional Odriísta; UNO), which ironically went
into alliance with the APRA as a voting coalition during
1963-1968, despite the fact that Odría had driven Haya
into exile earlier. After the progressive generals came
to power in 1968, Odría faded from public view in retirement. He died at age 77 on February 18, 1974, in
Lima.

OLMOS IRRIGATION PROJECT. The project at Olmos in
1919 pioneered modern irrigation-water farming in Peru,
launched by an agricultural experimentation station of
the government.

ORBEGOSO, LUIS JOSE. A general who in 1834 became
President of Peru after a military junta temporarily
prevented him from taking office.

ORDENANZAS DE TOLEDO. In 1574, Spain's viceroy in Peru,
Francisco de Toledo, collected all of the decrees and
laws about mining into a volume of ordinances. This
work, the Ordenanzas de Toledo, was approved into law
by King Philip II of Spain on February 7, 1574. The
mining industry was very important for the economy of
colonial Peru and for that of Spain also.

ORREGO, ANTENOR (1892-1960). A philosopher in the northern coastal city of Trujillo, he was prominent among Peruvian intellectuals.   In the 1920s, he wrote and lectured in favor of indigenismo, or Indianism, exalting the cultural heritage of Peru's Indians.

ORTEGA, JULIO.   Born in 1942 in Casma.   Author of nine widely-read books including drama, literary criticism, poetry, and novels.   In the 1960s and 1970s, Ortega was acclaimed as a Peruvian playwright.   After graduating from Catholic University in Lima, he taught Peruvian literature at Yale University and at the University of Texas at Austin.   Winner of a 1973-74 Guggenheim Foundation award, and winner of the National Prize for Theater Writing in 1968 and 1970.   Frequent contributor to international scholarly reviews.   His Teatro volume, published in 1965, includes eleven of his plays.   Since that time he has lived in Lima where he is Director of Publishing for the National Institute of Culture.

OVIEDO, JOSE MIGUEL.   Born in 1934 in Lima.   Received his doctorate in literature from Catholic University in Lima in 1961.   Has taught literature at Catholic and at San Marcos National Universities.   As Director of Cultural Extension for the National Engineering University, in September 1967 he organized the famous "Dialogues" held in Lima between Gabriel García Márquez, left-wing neo-Marxist writer from Colombia, and Mario Vargas Llosa, Peru's leading novelist of the 1960s and 1970s, from Arequipa, and a liberal critic of Marxian rigidity. The "Dialogues on Novels in Latin America" were widely reported throughout Latin America.

OXOTA.   The Quechuan word for a type of sandal consisting of a sole made of twisted vegetable cord and a rope thong, worn by Indians in the Andean villages.

-P-

PACASMAYO.   A town on the Pacific Coast in northern Peru, located in the Province of Pacasmayo within the Department of La Libertad.   Its municipal population in 1977 was estimated at 50,000, but Pacasmayo has had an importance as a transportation terminal for some time far out of proportion to its size.   It is the terminal for a railroad going eastward into the Andes to vital mining sites at Chilete.   Pacasmayo is a rest-stop on the paved

coastal highway linking Lima, far to the south, with
Talara and Tumbes to the north and the Ecuadorian
border. Pacasmayo has port facilities for fishing vessels and an airport.

PACHACAMAC see INCA

PACHAS TORRES, GUILLERMO. A legal expert who in 1965
in Lima published the Manual de resoluciones y formu-
larios en el procedimiento civil (Manual of Resolutions
and Formulas in Civil Procedure), a landmark summa-
tion of Peruvian civil law procedure codes, written
clearly and concisely in 191 pages.

PACIFIC, WAR OF THE. The war between Chile and Peru
allied with Bolivia during 1879-1884. Chile declared
war on Peru on April 3, 1879. The fundamental cause
was the increasing power of Chile and the weakness of
Peru and Bolivia, which had jurisdiction over valuable
nitrate lands. Peru and Bolivia seemed unable to develop these lands effectively and Chile was eager to do
so. By 1881, Chile had so overwhelmed Peruvian and
Bolivian troops that a politically divided Peru began to
seek a settlement. In October 1883, Peru signed the
Treaty of Ancón, recognizing Chilean sovereignty over
territory previously held by Peru and Bolivia.

PAIS, EL. The Lima daily newspaper which editorially led
the political attacks against President of Peru Andrés
A. Cáceres when he ran unopposed for the presidency
in March 1886. El País gave considerable space to the
views of the Democratic Party.

PAJA. The Spanish word for straw, "paja" in the northern
coastal towns also means a straw hat. In southern and
Andean cities, peasants wear wool hats and caps.

PALACIO. The Spanish word for "palace." Yet in most of
the Latin American republics, including Peru, it is the
official name for governmental buildings. The Palacio
Presidencial means the Presidential Building. A Palacio
Municipal should be translated as a Municipal Building
rather than "Municipal Palace."

PALMA, RICARDO. An outstanding literary critic and writer
and civic leader, who in October 1856 joined Manuel
Vivanco and Admiral Miguel Grau in the insurrection

against authoritarian decrees of President Ramón Castilla. However, Castilla then asserted that he supported a liberal 1856 Constitution and his decrees were merely a short-term device for preventing chaos. Compromises between Castilla and the Vivanco-Palma groups ensued.

PALMA UNIVERSITY. A private institution, the Universidad Ricardo Palma in Lima has developed an outstanding school of languages for professional translators and for business executives going into foreign trade. It also stresses business administration.

PALTA. The Quechuan word for the fruit known as an alligator pear or avocado in English, and as aguacate in Spanish. Considered a delicacy in various regions of Peru.

PAMPA. The Quechuan word for plain or flatland. This word, which originated in Peru during the Inca Empire, today is used by Spanish-speaking South Americans in general and is best known throughout the world as the name of the plains region of Argentina. The original "pampa" was corrupted by the Aymará Indians centuries ago in Bolivia into "bamba," and this usage exists today not only in Aymará culture in southern Peru and all of Bolivia but also in the suffix of geographic names in Bolivia (which was called Upper Peru before independence from Spain). Most famous such region and city in Bolivia perhaps is Cochabamba. At the other end of the old Inca Empire, to the north in present-day Ecuador, survive similar place names, such as Riobamba and Tomebamba.

PANDO, JOSE M. DE. José de Pando was chosen in 1827 by the great Liberator, Simón Bolívar, to be Minister of Government in Lima. Pando was born in 1787 in Lima, but as a young adult lived in Spain as a diplomat. He returned to Lima in 1823 and became a leader of political conservatives. He published a bi-weekly newspaper, La Verdad, during 1832 and 1833.

PANDO-NOBOA TREATY. A treaty between Peru and Ecuador signed on July 12, 1832, establishing an alliance for defense. In 1866, when Spain made an unsuccessful attempt to regain sovereignty in the coastal regions of Peru, Ecuador and Peru united in their defense against Spanish ships and troops under this treaty.

PARAMO. The high plains within the Andean Mountains, almost without trees and usually windswept.

PARDO, MANUEL. Born on August 9, 1834, in Lima, the
son of conservative writer Felipe Pardo. His early
schooling was in Chile. He returned to Lima in 1848,
entering the National University of San Carlos at age
fourteen. In 1850 he entered the University of Barce-
lona, Spain, later transferring to the University of Paris,
after perfecting his French. He returned to Peru in
1853 to launch a business career. As a writer, he became widely quoted as a champion of Peruvian nationalism. Minister of the Treasury in 1866. President of
the Lima Public Beneficence Society in 1868. Mayor of
Lima in 1869-1870. In October 1871 Peruvians elected
an Electoral College which in turn would choose a President of the republic. Pardo had founded the Civilista
Party and thus was its candidate. In May 1872 he was
elected as the first civilian President of Peru. He created public elementary schools, the faculty of political
and administrative sciences at San Marcos University,
and normal schools for women and for men, to train a
corps of public school teachers. In the election of 1866,
Pardo was succeeded in the presidency by the similarly
named Mariano Prado. Civilian Pardo had urged his
Civilista Party to elect General Prado because several
uprisings seemed to call for military leadership.

PARDO Y BARREDA, JOSE. Born in 1864, the son of Peru's
first full-term civilian president, Manuel Pardo. Presidential candidate of the Civilista Party in the 1904 election. A new Lima daily, La Prensa, founded in 1903,
opposed him and the longtime leading daily, El Comercio, supported the forty-year-old Pardo. During his administration (1904-1908), the budget of the Ministry of
Instruction and Justice doubled, as did the number of
primary school students. After his term, Pardo lived
in Europe from 1908 to 1914. He served a second
term as President during 1915-1919.

PAREJA-VIVANCO TREATY. The treaty which Peru and
Spain signed in January 1865. In April 1864, naval
ships of Spain seized the Chincha Islands, 100 miles
from the Peruvian shore, southwest of Callao. After
the United States and most other Latin American nations
protested this attempt to colonize, Spain ordered Admiral José Pareja to sign a treaty with Peruvian Gen-

eral Manuel Vivanco, withdrawing all Spanish personnel
and ships from Peru's coastal or territorial waters.

PARIÑAS see LA BREA OILFIELDS

PARTIDO APRISTA PERUANO. The American Popular Rev-
olutionary Alliance (Alianza Popular Revolucionaria
Americana; APRA), founded in 1924. A 1956 Electoral
Law against international parties prompted APRA to
change its name to the Peruvian Aprista Party or PAP.
In 1977 it got certified for the 1978 and 1980 elections.

PARTIDO COMUNISTA PERUANO. The Peruvian Communist
Party, or PCP, began in 1928 as the Peruvian Socialist
Party, taking its present name in 1930. It has a pro-
Soviet Union policy but a smaller PCP, which is pro-
Chinese, uses the same name and initials. Since Au-
gust 1975, the PCP has been allowed to function freely.
In 1977 it was certified for the 1978 and 1980 elections.

PARTIDO DEMOCRATA CRISTIANO. The Christian Democratic
Party, or PDC, was founded in 1955. It was active in
Congress in a coalition with Popular Action during 1963-
1968. It was certified in 1977 for the 1978 and 1980
elections.

PARTIDO SOCIALISTA REVOLUCIONARIO. The Socialist
Revolutionary Party, or PSR, was organized in 1975.
Antonio Meza Cuadra heads it as secretary general. It
was certified in 1977 for the 1978 and 1980 elections.

PARTIES, POLITICAL. One Peruvian political party does
not use the word "party" in its title: Acción Popular
or Popular Action, founded by Fernando Belaúnde in
1956. It was certified in 1977 for the 1978 and 1980
elections. One other political party did not use the
word "party" during its active period of 1962-1968. It
was the National Odriísta Union (Union Nacional Odriísta;
UNO). Former dictator and president General Manuel
Odría founded the UNO and it functioned in an alliance
with the Apristas in Congress during 1963-1968.

PARTY OF THE PEOPLE. The name temporarily given to
the American Popular Revolutionary Alliance (APRA) in
1945 to satisfy electoral law regulations then put into
force.

PASCO.   One of the twenty-four Departments of administration into which Peru is divided geographically.   The Department of Pasco in turn is subdivided into three Provinces, one of which bears the name Province of Pasco.
In this region the famous Cerro de Pasco mining camps
are found.

PASCO, CERRO DE.   The corporation Cerro de Pasco was
a private mining corporation owned by United States investors until the military government of President Juan
Velasco expropriated it in January 1974.   It then came
under the governmental agency Centromín.

PATRIA.   The newspaper La Patria in 1878 became the voice
of the politicians led by Nicolás de Piérola and of those
advocating pro-clerical policies for Peru.

PAZ SOLDAN, JOSE.   Minister of Foreign Relations under
President Ramón Castilla, José Paz Soldán organized
the foreign service into Peru's first professional corps
of diplomats, instituting short courses in international
law, protocol, and foreign languages.   During 1845-1851
the minister upgraded Peru's foreign service from one
of the most disorganized in South America to a position
of leadership rivaling the foreign service of Chile.

PEREZ GODOY, RICARDO.   Born in 1905.   Graduated from
the Escuela Militar and commissioned in the Army.
Rose through the ranks from lieutenant to division general.   In June 1962, he led the military group which
seized power for a one-year period, nullifying the disputed indeterminate election results of the presidential
race, which had split three ways.   One year later, the
military junta caretaker government, in which General
Nicolás Lindley had succeeded Pérez Godoy as President in March 1963, held elections again.   The same
candidates who had run in June 1962 were on the ballot
in June 1963.   Fernando Belaúnde won and was inaugurated as President on July 28, 1963, and Pérez Godoy
retired from public life.   During the 1962-63 period,
he established Peru's Institute of Planning (Instituto de
Planificación), a governmental Housing Bank (Banco de
la Vivienda), and a new housing agency to carry out
slum-clearance projects, the National Housing Board
(Junta Nacional de la Vivienda).   All of these entities
survived from his brief term throughout the 1963-1968
Belaúnde administration, the 1968-1975 Velasco administration and the 1975-1980 Morales administration.

PERUANIDAD. Víctor Andrés Belaúnde, writer and uncle of
Peruvian President Fernando Belaúnde (1963-1968), wrote
a book called Peruanidad, published in 1957, asserting
that "Peruvianity" meant that Spanish culture had ab-
sorbed the best of Indian culture into a distinct Peruvian culture.

PERUVIAN STEAMSHIP COMPANY. In 1906 Augusto B.
Leguía organized the Peruvian Steamship Company (Compañía Peruana de Vapores) to carry cargo to and from
the port of Callo.

PESCAPERU see FISHERIES REFORM LAW

PETROPERU see INTERNATIONAL PETROLEUM COMPANY

PEZET, JUAN ANTONIO. Juan Antonio Pézet was elected
Vice-President when General Miguel San Román was
elected President of Peru in 1862. On April 3, 1863,
San Román died after a long illness, and Pézet became
President. In November 1866, he was ousted by mili-
tary rivals.

PEZUELA, JOAQUIN DE. Succeeded José de Abscal as Viceroy of Peru in 1816. In late August 1820, General
José de San Martín, having liberated Chile, commanded
a 4,500-man army, sailing in a Chilean fleet manned
by 1,600 sailors and marines under Chilean officers.
Landing at the southern port of Pisco on September 8,
San Martín began distributing weapons to 15,000 Peruvian recruits. Viceroy Pezuela--fatally hesitating although he commanded 23,000 trained Spanish troops--
finally engaged the Peruvian-Chilean forces in several
battles. On December 24, 1820, the Marquis of Torre
Tagle, the Peruvian-born intendant of Trujillo, joined
the cause of independence, lowering the morale of some
of the royalist leaders. By 1821, Pezuela had been replaced as viceroy. On July 28, 1821, San Martín proclaimed Peru to be independent of Spain, but the last
Spanish soldiers did not leave until after their defeat on
December 9, 1824, at the battle of Ayacucho.

PICHINCHA. A Quechuan word meaning "boiling mountain"
or volcano.

PIEROLA, AMADEO DE. Son of Peruvian President Nicolás
de Piérola (1895-1899). Amadeo de Piérola led a group
which stormed the National Palace and made Augusto B.

Leguía their prisoner on May 29, 1909. They marched
President Leguía down the street, then released him,
in a strange and brief revolt against his policies.

PIEROLA, NICOLAS DE. Born on January 5, 1839, in Arequipa. Died on June 23, 1913, age 74. Statesman and
politician who was dominant in Peruvian political life for
three decades, serving not only as the "Democratic Caudillo" President during 1895-1899, but also as founder
of the Democratic Party, and a debater, essayist, writer on every major public issue. Founded the newspaper
El Tiempo in 1864 to defend policies of President Juan
Pézet. In 1869 became Minister of the Treasury, re-
signing in 1871. Urged military preparedness, antici-
pating the War of the Pacific attack by Chile in 1879.
Became acting President of Peru on December 23, 1879.
When Chileans occupied Lima on January 17, 1881,
Piérola withdrew his headquarters from Lima to Ayacucho, until the Chileans withdrew in 1884. In Lima,
an assembly ignored Piérola's presidential claims and
named Francisco García Calderón as President. Piérola
had his followers found the Democratic Party in Lima
in 1884 during his absence. Elected in July 1895,
Piérola served a constitutional term into 1899.

PIFANO. A Quechuan word for a wooden fife, carved from
reed, with six finger holes, ranging only one octave.

PISCO. A city on the Pacific coast 194 kilometers south of
Lima on the Pan American coastal highway. Pisco has
good harbor facilities for fishing fleets and cargo ships,
an airport, and a railroad yard for freight trains shut-
tling 73 kilometers southward to the city of Icá. The
city of Pisco is in the Province of Pisco and the city
of Icá is in the Province of Icá; both Provinces are
within the Department of Icá.

PISCO SOUR. A brandy mixed drink popular with Peruvians
and foreign tourists alike. It originated in the city of
Pisco but it has become a mainstay of fashionable bars
and restaurants in Lima and elsewhere.

PITI. A Quechuan word meaning a small quantity.

PIURA. One of the twenty-four administrative Departments
into which Peru is divided geographically. The Department of Piura is subdivided into seven Provinces, of

which the Province of Piura is one. Within that Province lies the city of Piura, in northern Peru, approximately 100 kilometers due south of the Ecuadorian border, and 55 kilometers inland from the Pacific coast. Piura is on the Pan American Highway and has an airport.

PIUS XII. Born as Eugenio Pacelli in Italy in 1876. Died in Rome as Pope Pius XII in 1958. Succeeded by Pope John XXIII (Angelo Roncalli, born 1881, died 1963), who in late 1958 began modernizing the strictly traditional atmosphere of the Vatican. The change engendered debate in Peru as to the extent of governmental patronage for the Catholic Church in Peru. By 1963, when Pope John was succeeded by Pope Paul VI (Giovanni Montini born 1897), some of the traditional entities in Peruvian public life had become secularized. For example, until 1958, most charitable trust funds had been administered by bishops, but now are administered by bankers.

PIZARRO, FRANCISCO. Born in 1470 in Extremadura, Spain. Killed by political rival Spaniards in his governor's palace in Lima in 1541. Son of an army officer and a servant girl, born out of wedlock. A swineherd as a youth. No formal education, but he learned to read and write rudimentary Spanish. Sailed to Cuba seeking fame and fortune. In 1520, when he was fifty years old, considerably older than Hernán Cortés, who had just conquered the Aztec Empire in Mexico, Pizarro heard Spanish sailors tell of another Indian realm far to the south which rivaled the wealth of the Aztecs. In 1524, Pizarro organized his expedition. In 1531 he sailed southward from Panama with 180 men and 27 horses, landing on the coast of Ecuador; then traveled southward to Tumbés in northern Peru, where he learned that the Inca Empire was divided in a civil war between half-brothers, Atahualpa and Huáscar. As conqueror of Peru, Pizarro created his capital of Lima on January 6, 1535, away from the Inca capital deep in the Andes at Cuzco.

PIZARRO, GONZALO. Born in 1506 in Trujillo, Spain. Died on April 12, 1548, in Cuzco. Brother of Francisco Pizarro, Gonzalo participated in the conquest of Peru.

PIZARRO, HERNANDO. Born in Spain. Brother of Francisco and Gonzalo Pizarro. Hernando served as his brother

Francisco's messenger back and forth to the royal court
in Spain from the conqueror's office in Lima.

PIZARRO, PEDRO. Born in 1499 in Spain. Died on February
9, 1587, in Quito, Ecuador. First cousin of Francisco
Pizarro, conqueror of Peru. Historian of the Spanish
conquests of Peru and Ecuador.

PLAN DEL PERU. Published by Manuel Lorenzo de Vidaurre
in 1823, the Plan del Perú urged the parliament of Spain
to grant Peru a measure of autonomy, not for the masses
but for the aristocrats or leaders who administered the
viceroyalty in the audiencia, or administrative court in
Lima. Born in 1782 in Lima, Vidaurre was chosen by
Viceroyalty officials to represent Peru in the Cortes,
or parliament, in Cádiz in Spain. It was there that he
wrote and published his plan.

PLAN TUPAC AMARU. Named after an Inca prince to project an image of national heritage and development, the
Plan Tupac Amaru was drafted in 1976, then debated
and refined during the spring of 1977 by the Council of
Presidential Advisors (COAP) and the cabinet ministers
of President Francisco Morales Bermúdez. In its final
form it was published by the government on October 9,
1977. The plan outlines programs running into the 1980s,
to develop the economy, raise living standards, increase
literacy and industrialization, and develop elected civilian
leaders who will respond to ongoing social reforms and
modernization. Critics of the military government's
practice of "guiding" the mass media had debated at
length whether to try to get a reversal of the 1974 decree socializing the newspapers and broadcasting stations
in the hands of workers' societies, but in the final draft
that basic change in the Peruvian communication system
remained.

PLAZA DE ARMAS. The central square in downtown Lima
which has been site of Peruvian government since Francisco Pizarro established it in 1535. On the northern
edge of this plaza lies the Presidential Palace, wherein
are located the offices of the President and his key staff
members. Just to the west is the statue of Pizarro
astride his horse. Along the eastern edge of this plaza
is the national Cathedral and headquarters of the Catholic Church. Along the western edge is the Lima Municipal Building and the exclusive Union Club, a private

facility for aristocrats. Retail firms and corporation offices occupy colonial-style arcaded buildings along the southern edge of the plaza.

PLAZA DE SAN MARTIN. The second most important square in Peru, the San Martín Plaza, named for liberator General José de San Martín, has his statue at its very center. To the west is the famed Hotel Bolívar, longtime luxury-level hotel whose tea room remains a late afternoon gathering place for old-line Lima aristocrats. Motion picture theaters, airline offices, and restaurants line the peripheries of this plaza.

POINCARE, RAYMOND. Distinguished jurist and writer in the field of international law, Raymond Poincaré in 1933 wrote at length about the seizure in September 1932 of Leticia, a Colombian port on the Amazon River, by a group of Peruvians. The legal reference, International Opinion and the Leticia Controversy, published in Washington, prompted Peru in 1933 to withdraw from Leticia.

POLICIA INVESTIGADOR PERUANO. The Policía Investigador Peruano or PIP (Peruvian Investigative Police), constitutes the detective corps and intelligence corps of the republic. Municipal-level police, which since 1976 have included women, are restricted to traffic control and minor duties. Other uniformed police, as well as PIP officers in civilian attire, are national, not local, and come under the direction of the Minister of the Interior.

POLITICAL PARTIES see PARTIES, POLITICAL

PONCE, CLEMENTE. Legal commentator and jurist who wrote Límites entre el Ecuador y el Perú, published in Madrid in 1907, then in La Paz, Bolivia, in 1910, and in an English-language translation, Boundaries Between Ecuador and Peru, in 1910 in Washington, D. C. This book became a noted reference in international negotiations between the two nations.

PONCE, HUMBERTO. Humberto Ponce was Minister of the Treasury in the cabinet of President Manuel Odría during 1950-1955, and the target of numerous charges of graft. Ponce became wealthy after many large landowners and industrialists received tax reductions through legal technicalities personally interpreted by the minister.

PONCE-CASTRO PROTOCOL.   An agreement signed by Peru
and Ecuador on June 21, 1924, providing that the two
nations should begin direct negotiations in Washington,
D. C. over their boundary disputes.

POPULAR ACTION.   Acción Popular, or Popular Action, is
a political party founded in 1956 by Fernando Belaúnde,
who became the AP candidate for president in the 1956
and the nullified 1962 elections, and again in the 1963
election, which he won.   Belaúnde served from July 28,
1963, until ousted by the military on October 3, 1968.
His AP teamed with the Christian Democratic Party
members of the Senate and Chamber of Deputies during
1963-1968 as a coalition, balanced by the rival alliance
of the Apristas and the Odriístas, giving Peru during
the five-year period four active political parties but in
a sense a two-party Congress, with the four parties
functioning in their respective tandems.

POPULAR COOPERATION.   The social service program of
the administration of President Fernando Belaúnde during 1963-1968, also known as the Interministerial Commission program.   Young Peruvian volunteers worked
in slum neighborhoods of cities and impoverished villages
on community development projects, paralleling in a
loose sense the Vista and Peace Corps volunteers of
the United States.

PORRAS BARRENECHEA, RAUL (1877-1960).   Historian,
jurist, legal commentator.   In 1926 he published the
definitive Historia de los límites del Perú, a noted reference giving the detailed history of boundary problems
which have confronted Peru from colonial into modern
times.   In 1928, Raúl Porras Barrenechea delivered an
address commemorating the centennial of the birthday
of Toribio Pacheco, codifying author of early 19th-cen-
tury Peruvian civil law.   It was published as a 41-page
booklet in 1928 and has become a key capsule guide to
scholars researching the works of Pacheco.

PORTAL, MAGDA.   Longtime leader of the women's groups
within the American Popular Revolutionary Alliance
(APRA), Magda Portal resigned as Aprista women's
leader in 1956, in a dispute over policies.

PORTALES, DIEGO.   Conservative political leader, who commanded rebel troops in 1836 in a brief revolt against

liberal General Andrés Santa Cruz in southern Peru,
and was killed in battle in 1837.

PORTETE DE TARQUI, BATTLE OF. In February 1829,
    Colombia's troops defeated Peruvian troops inside Co-
    lombia not far from the disputed Peruvian-Colombian
    border. Victorious Colombians were commanded by
    General José de Sucre. Since Spanish colonial times,
    Peruvian leaders had considered Ecuador, Upper Peru
    (renamed Bolivia after independence), and southern Co-
    lombia as traditionally belonging to Peru because in the
    pre-Hispanic era, these lands were ruled by the Inca
    Empire. This attitude provoked many boundary disputes
    between Peru and its neighbors during the 19th and early
    20th centuries.

PORTOTO. A Quechuan word for beans, used by Indians in
    northern Peru but not in southern regions.

PRADO, JAVIER (1871-1921). A leading intellectual and writer.
    His essays stressed that the practice of chewing the
    coca leaf had destroyed the Indians psychologically and
    prevented their social and economic advancement.

PRADO, JORGE. Brother of writer and political commenta-
    tor Javier Prado, Jorge Prado in 1914 also became as
    active in the Civilismo (Civilianism) political movement
    as his more famous brother. The Prados opposed Pres-
    ident Guillermo Billinghurst's increasing assaults on con-
    stitutional standards in 1913 and 1914, and helped oust
    Billinghurst on February 4, 1914. In 1921, Jorge Prado
    went into exile to protest the tyrannical activities of
    Minister of the Interior Germán Leguía, a cousin of
    President Augusto B. Leguía, and lived in various Euro-
    pean cities. His brother, Javier Prado, who had be-
    come president of San Marcos University, died of na-
    tural causes in 1921 before he could join Jorge in exile.
    Jorge Prado became Prime Minister of the cabinet of
    President Oscar R. Benavides in 1933. He was the
    candidate for president of the National Front (Frente
    Nacional), a party founded to advance his candidacy, in
    the 1936 elections, whose results were nullified by Pres-
    ident Benavides, who continued in office into 1939.

PRADO, JORGE DEL. Born in Lima. As a youth, active
    in the Juventud Comunista Peruana (Peruvian Communist
    Youth). Active in the Political Committee activities of

the Peruvian Communist Party (Partido Comunista Peruano; PCP). Became Secretary General of the PCP in 1960 and has been periodically re-elected by the PCP Central Committee. In 1978 del Prado again was reaffirmed by the Central Committee to continue as its leader. The government of President Morales Bermúdez decided in November 1977 to recognize the PCP as a lawful party. In the election of June 18, 1978, in which five million Peruvians voted for 100 members of a Constituent Assembly as the first step in returning the government from military to civilian rule by 1980, the PCP captured 6 per cent of the total votes cast, to gain six seats in that assembly. Anti-Marxist APRA with 35 seats and the Popular Christian Party (Partido Popular Cristiano) with 27 seats, could dominate the multiparty assembly. One of the six PCP seats went to del Prado.

PRADO, MANUEL. Born April 21, 1889, son of Mariano I. Prado, and brother of Javier and Jorge Prado, in a family of political leaders and influential writers in the national life of Peru. Died August 15, 1967. Professional career: banker. Elected President of Peru in 1939, for a first term during 1939-1945. Supported by the Apristas as a coalition conservative candidate of several groups, Prado legalized APRA, which had been outlawed. Wartime ally of the United States against Germany, Italy, and Japan during 1942-1945. In the 1956 election, Prado became the candidate of the National Coalition Party, and won. Second presidential term, July 1956 to June 1962. In 1958, Prado shocked Catholic Peru by having a three-bishop committee annul his 43-year marriage so that the 69-year-old Prado could marry a 36-year-old woman in the Catholic Church. During his second term, the government ended any hint of censorship or news management or "guidance" of the media. The 1956-1962 period was the golden age of press freedom in Peru. Even at the height of editorial denunciations of his marriage annulment, Prado never attempted to shut off the severe criticism with the stand-by presidential powers he had.

PRADO, MARIANO IGNACIO. General Mariano Ignacio Prado, twice President of Peru, was the father of three national leaders, Javier, Jorge, and Manuel Prado. In 1866, Mariano Prado became dictator of Peru when President Juan Pézet was exiled. After liberals promulgated the Constitution of 1867, the Prado dictatorship was overthrown. In 1876, Prado was elected President and had to lead Peru in its War of the Pacific against Chile in 1879. On December 18, 1879, he sailed for Europe to obtain loans and ships for national defense. On December 21, a group suspicious that General Prado had fled the country in cowardice proclaimed Nicolás de Piérola as President. Prado thus lost the presidency and did not gain the European loans Peru needed.

PRENSA, LA. The Lima daily newspaper La Prensa was founded in 1901. In the 1904 presidential campaign, it supported Nicolás de Piérola, while the older, more established rival daily, El Comercio, supported José Pardo, who won. By the 1950s, El Comercio had become the editorial voice of the exporters, the landowning wealthy families. La Prensa had become the editorial voice of the importers, the newer middle class and upper class industrialists and retailers. Both dailies remained conservative and both were expropriated by the military government of President Juan Velasco under the decree of July 29, 1974. The government had forced La Prensa publisher Pedro Beltrán to sell his stock in the newspaper in 1972 to the 508 employees of the paper and allowed his nephew to remain as publisher until 1974.

PRIALE, RAMON. In 1956, Ramón Prialé became the chief campaign orator in Lima for the Apristas, in the presidential election won by conservative coalition candidate Manuel Prado.

PROVINCIA. The Spanish word for province. In Peru, the republic is divided administratively into twenty-four geographical Departments. Each department is subdivided into provinces. Unlike the federal republic of the United States, in which each of the fifty states exercises states' rights, in the unitary or centralized republic of Peru, departments and provinces are mere geographical extensions of the national capital in Lima. The president of the republic and his cabinet ministers set the provincial and local (municipal) standards, and choose the officials for each department and each province within the department to carry out national laws and programs.

PUCALLPA. Pucallpa is a small city on the Ucayali River in easternmost Peru in the Department of Loreto. It

lies approximately 120 kilometers from the Brazilian
border, deep in a jungle. No land connections run eastward. Westward, however, an oiled, gravel highway
connects Pucallpa through the Andean mountain passes
to Tingo María. Pucallpa has an airport which links it
by air to Lima.

PUENTE, JOSE DE LA. A conservative historian who published several studies of Peruvian culture from the point
of view of the Catholic Church leadership in 1964 and
1965.

PUNO. A city in southeastern Peru facing Lake Titicaca.
From the docks of Puno daily and nightly cargo and passenger ships cross Lake Titicaca to the Bolivian shore
at Guaqui, a short highway or train ride from La Paz,
capital of Bolivia. Puno has an airport, and connects
via railroad northward to Cuzco and southwestward to
Arequipa. Puno and Arequipa also connect by highway.

PUNO, DEPARTMENT OF. Puno is the name of a city, and
also the name of one of the twenty-four administrative
Departments of the republic. The Department of Puno
is subdivided into nine provinces, one of which is the
Province of Puno, which contains the city of Puno. In
the 1972 Census, the Province of Puno had 124,823 inhabitants, most of them in the city of Puno.

PURUHA. The Indian tribe which ruled the Kingdom of Quito
until 1487 A.D. , when the Peruvian Indians from the
Inca Empire conquered and annexed the Kingdom of
Quito (present-day Ecuador).

PUTUMAYO RIVER. A tributary of the Amazon River, which
forms part of the border between Ecuador and Colombia.
Peru claimed the area until 1922, when, at the urging
of the United States, Peru and Colombia signed the Sal-
omón-Lozano Treaty, giving the narrow jungle corridor
along the Putumayo River completely to Colombia.

PUZUN. A Quechuan word meaning abdomen of a human or
of an animal. Most commonly used to denote the belly
of a llama, an alpaca, or a vicuña.

-Q-

QUECHUA. The name of the Indians and of their language.

The Quechua Indians were the largest group within the ancient Inca Empire before the conquest by the Spaniards in 1532, and today remain a larger group than any other Indian group in the entire Andes, the mountain range stretching from Colombia through Peru and Bolivia into northern Argentina and Chile.

QUENA. A wooden flute played by Quechua and Aymará Indians throughout Peru, Bolivia, and southern Ecuador.

QUESADA, JOSE. José Quesada was a presidential candidate of the Revolutionary Union in the election of 1939, in which Manuel Prado won the presidency.

QUILCA. The Quechuan word for scribe or writer or minor political official. Among bilingual Peruvians, the word "quilca" has become a slang word for attorney, and among Spanish-speaking Peruvians it has come to mean unethical or "shyster" lawyer.

QUILICO. A Quechuan word widely used by Spanish-speaking Peruvians also. It means a hawk in some areas and a falcon as a specific species in other regions.

QUINOA. A quinoa is a plant growing high in the Andean Mountains. Its seed is used as a cereal food by the Indians. It has high protein content. It grows wild at altitudes more than 8,000 feet above sea-level.

QUISQUIS. A general of the Inca Empire army under Prince Atahualpa. In 1532 A.D. he defeated the army of rival claimant to the Inca throne, Atahualpa's half-brother, Prince Huáscar. The Spaniards soon thereafter conquered both armies.

QUITO. Capital city of the republic of Ecuador, and capital of the pre-Hispanic Kingdom of Quito, part of the Inca Empire before the conquest of the Andean region by the Spaniards.

-R-

RADA y GAMIO, PEDRO J. Pedro J. Rada y Gamio, prime minister in the cabinet of President Augusto B. Leguía from 1927 to the 1930 ouster of Leguía. Rada was a moderate and not associated with any of the stern measures of the Leguía regime.

RADIO NACIONAL. The government's radio station, Radio
   Nacional, was organized in 1935 by Peruvian President
   Oscar Benavides through a contract with the Marconi
   Company. Through that Marconi link, Nacional traces
   its heritage to Peru's first full-time daily radio station,
   OAX, in 1925, and to the pioneer amateur radio stations
   of Callao of 1923.

RADIO NEWS. News reporting over radio in Peru was pioneered by the government station, Radio Nacional, after
   that station first went on the air in 1935. By the 1970s,
   Nacional consisted not only of medium-, short-, and long-
   wave transmitters in Lima, but also several repeater
   transmitters in the provincial cities, giving the republic
   its most extensive radio network. Nacional also broad-
   casts on the frequency modulation band in Lima. In
   November 1971, presidential decree law 19020, the General Law of Telecommunications, permitted the government to purchase 25 per cent ownership of all privately-
   owned radio stations in Peru and 51 per cent of all privately-owned television stations.

RADIO VICTORIA. According to audience surveys in the
   1960s and before the 1971 expropriations, Radio Victoria
   in Lima drew the largest audiences of any private radio
   station.

RAPHAEL AND SONS. The London corporation which in 1876
   signed an agreement with the government of Peru for
   the exporting of guano to Britain, to be sold in Europe
   as fertilizer. President Mariano Prado thereby postponed
   an extreme financial crisis until 1879, with the infusion
   of English pounds into the treasury for the Peruvian exports.

RAVINES, EUDOCIO. In 1929, Eudocio Ravines helped José
   Carlos Mariátegui found the Socialist Party of Peru,
   which later changed its name to the Communist Party
   of Peru. When the Communists in Peru flip-flopped
   overnight in their policy towards World War II, Ravines
   became disillusioned. Before Germany attacked Russia,
   Hitler and Stalin had a non-aggression pact and the Moscow line urged North and South Americans to remain
   neutral while the Nazis conquered Western European
   nations, one by one. But in 1941, as soon as Germany
   invaded the Soviet Union, the Moscow-sponsored "peace"
   movement changed overnight to an intervention movement,

with the Communist Party of Peru following suit. Ravines realized that the national aspirations he had for
Peru could not coexist with a party whose first loyalty
was to the Soviet Union, not to Peru. By 1950, Ravines
had matured into an articulate anti-Marxist, speaking to
conservative and moderate groups about the tactics Communists use to try to maneuver political crises to their
advantage.

REBELDE   see   REVOLUTIONARY LEFTIST MOVEMENT

REBOZO   see   MACANA

REFRESCO   see   FRESCO

REGIONAL PERUVIAN LABOR FEDERATION.   The Federa-
    ción Obrera Regional Peruana, or Regional Peruvian
    Labor Federation, was founded in 1919 to campaign for
    an eight-hour day for workers in all occupations, after
    the government stipulated an eight-hour work day only
    for workers in manufacturing and mining. Some indus-
    trial workers did not get the eight-hour work day until
    the 1920s, and others not until the late 1930s.

REPUBLICA, LA.   In September 1930, leftist politicians
    founded the newspaper La República to support editor-
    ially the Communist Party of Peru. In October 1930,
    the Socialist Party of Peru was founded and began draw-
    ing readers away from La República, which declined into
    a weekly of small circulation.

RESTORATIVE REVOLUTION.   On October 27, 1948, mili-
    tary leaders under General Manuel Odría seized power
    from civilian President José Bustamante, labeling their
    assumption of power the "restorative revolution," although
    the Odría administration from then until mid-1956 made
    no revolutionary changes and merely restored public or-
    der at the expense of the civil rights of many groups.

RETAILING.   Modern marketing techniques in retail sales
    dramatically increased in Lima and in Peru's few other
    large cities in the 1960s after Sears del Perú, a sub-
    sidiary of the Sears Roebuck department store chain of
    the United States, expanded its shopping center in the
    Lima suburb of San Isidro, and helped popularize credit
    card usage among the middle class. By the 1970s, the
    old-style merchandising, copied for decades from the

French merchants of the Bon Marché chain, had been superseded by North American retailing methods, especially in advertising and styling.

REVISTAS. The revistas, or magazines, of Peru have varied through the years. Some have been short-lived political pamphlets and some have been long-lived literary gazettes. Few have been national media of communications, with such exceptions as Sieta Días, the English-language Peruvian Times, which since 1975 has been called the Lima Times, and the news magazine Caretas (see CARETAS). The last-named was founded in 1950, suppressed for a while by the military government of President Juan Velasco, and since 1975 has again been a popular magazine, frequently sold out at news stands the day after publication each week.

REVOLUTIONARY LEFTIST MOVEMENT. The Movimiento de Izquierda Revolucionaria (MIR), or Revolutionary Leftist Movement, began in Peru as a Communist-front called Rebelde (or "Rebel") in 1960. Receiving funds from Fidel Castro's Cuba, the MIR later was helped by leftist guerrilla Hugo Blanco, who subsequently went into exile rather than serve a prison term for killing three police officers. MIR violence of the 1960s subsided in the 1970s as the military government arrested or deported MIR leaders.

REYNOSO, OSWALDO. Born in 1932 in Arequipa and educated in Lima, a writer who helped initiate the urban narrative in Peru. He taught at secondary and preparatory schools in Lima, then at the National Normal School, and then at the National University of San Marcos. He was a co-director of the magazine Narración after its founding in 1966. His volume of short stories, Los inocentes, published in 1961, was re-issued in 1966 with the title Lima en rock. His novel En octubre was published in 1965.

RIBEYRO, JULIO RAMON. Born on August 31, 1929, in Lima. Law student at Catholic University in Lima during 1946-1952. In 1952 he won a scholarship to Spain. Since 1960, Julio Ramón Ribeyro has resided in Paris where he is Minister of Peru to UNESCO and an editor of Latin American news for the French News Agency (Agence France Presse; AFP). His 1960 novel Crónica de San Gabriel has been published in Spanish, Polish,

Dutch, and German editions. His 1958 <u>Cuentos</u> won the
1959 National Novel Prize in Peru.

RICHTER PRADA, PEDRO. Born on January 4, 1920, in
    Ayachucho. Married Laura Valdivia, a descendant of
    the conquistador Valdivia family of the 1530s. Descended
    from a German great-grandfather patrilinially, and ma-
    trilinially from the Pradas, an old-line Peruvian family
    tracing back to early colonial times. Graduated from
    the Escuela Militar at Chorrillos and commissioned in
    the Army in January 1946. Student at the Armored Of-
    ficer Advanced Course of the U.S. Army at Fort Knox,
    Kentucky, during 1955-1956. Student at the Escuela Su-
    perior de Guerra in 1952-1953. Graduated from the
    Center for Higher Military Studies (CAEM), Peru's think
    tank for officers, in 1965. He served as military at-
    taché at the Peruvian Embassy in La Paz, Bolivia, in
    1961-1962. During 1966, he was director of public re-
    lations for the Peruvian Army. In 1970 he became a
    member of the Council of Presidential Advisors (COAP),
    helping President Juan Velasco formulate major policies.
    In January 1971, he was appointed Director of the Na-
    tional Intelligence Service, serving until his appointment
    on May 18, 1971 as Minister of the Interior. In August
    1971, he raised the salary of police officers and, as In-
    terior Minister and therefore head of the police, forced
    from active duty those police known to be bribed by nar-
    cotics smugglers. Richter Prada then staged the larg-
    est and most successful raid ever held on the headquar-
    ters of organized crime in Peru, demolishing the center
    from which cocaine and other narcotics were illegally
    shipped to the United States and Europe. During the
    administration of President Francisco Morales Bermúdez,
    Richter Prada served in administrative posts for the
    army. In 1978 he was chairman of the armed forces
    joint chiefs of staff.

RIMAC. River on which the capital, Lima, is situated.

RIVA AGÜERO, JOSE. A descendant of the independence
    leader of 1810-1823, namesake José Riva Agüero in
    1932 founded an extremist right-wing group within the
    Catholic Church, and then broke it away into the Peru-
    vian Fascist Brotherhood. Riva embraced Hitler's ha-
    tred of everything Jewish, denounced capitalism, pro-
    moted national socialism. When Riva insisted that his
    followers address him as the "Marquis of Aulestia,"

some of them resigned from his group. After he appeared at a reception at a private club wearing a dress, he was committed to a rest home under a psychiatrist's care for six months. His fascist group evaporated after Peru joined the allies and declared war on Hitler's Germany in 1942.

RIVA AGÜERO, JOSE DE LA. In 1810, José de la Riva Agüero became one of the first Peruvians publicly to advocate independence from Spain. In February 1823, Congress designated Riva as Peru's first President of the Republic. When Spanish troops returned to Lima in June 1823, Riva and his administration retreated to Callao. Soon the Congress welcomed General Antonio de Sucre of Venezuela as a liberator and Riva withdrew from power and from the Lima-Callao area.

ROCA, ERASMO (1893-1963). Chairman of the National Commission of Land Ownership Claims of Peru in 1919. He sought interviews with dozens of Indian leaders to help residents of Andean villages establish claims to their traditional small farm lands.

RODO, JOSE ENRIQUE. Born on July 15, 1872, in Montevideo, Uruguay. Died in Palermo, Italy, on May 1, 1917, while serving as war correspondent for Montevideo newspapers. Rodó exerted enormous influence on Peruvian intellectuals through his book Ariel, published in 1900. In it, he warned Latin America that its enthusiasm for materialism as symbolized in U.S. technology could rob Latin Americans of spiritual goals found in Hispanic literature and culture. Paradoxically, in various other essays, Rodó praised United States industry and enterprise for bringing North Americans a higher standard of living, creature comforts, and free public education. But anti-Yankee intellectuals in Peru have consistently cited Ariel as a philosophical indictment of North America. Rodó dropped out of secondary school to support himself and became a self-taught writer and philosopher by reading at the Ateneo Library in Montevideo. After his death as a correspondent on a World War I battlefield, several Peruvian and Uruguayan institutions posthumously awarded him degrees or "alumnus" status.

RODRIGUEZ, CESAR A. During the 1920s César A. Rodríguez was a popular poet and writer for Peruvian periodicals.

RODRIGUEZ FIGUEROA, LEONIDAS.   Born in 1920 in Cuzco.
Graduated from the Escuela Militar and commissioned
in the infantry in January 1944.   Promoted to brigadier
general on January 1, 1970.   A member of the "inner
circle" of advisors of President Juan Velasco during
1969-1975, having been an original member of the Council of Presidential Advisors (COAP).   From 1970 to 1972
was commanding general of the 1st Armored Division in
Lima.   He then became Chief of SINAMOS, or Sistema
Nacional de Apoyo de Movilización Social (National System of Help of Social Mobilization), the government's
agency for coordination of grassroots efforts for all the
reform programs instituted since 1968.   In January 1974,
he was reassigned as commanding general of the military
region of Lima.   On June 18 he was deported after voting in the constituent assembly election, on charges of
promoting violence.

ROMERO, EMILIO.   Born in 1899.   Geographer and economist.
Wrote extensively on the practice among Indians of chew-
ing coca leaves.   By the 1950s Romero's essays were
insisting that this addiction was no more harmful to the
Indians of the Andes than cigarette smoking was to North
Americans.

ROMUALDO, ALEJANDRO.   Born on December 19, 1926, in
Trujillo.   Educated at the National University of San
Marcos.   Widely traveled in Asia, Africa, Europe, and
Latin America.   Since 1975, Romualdo has been Direc-
tor of Theater and Cinema for the National Institute of
Culture in Lima.   Considered one of the major poets of
Peru of the 1960s and 1970s, he has had nine volumes
of poems published.   His Cuarto mundo in 1972 received
notice throughout Latin American literary circles.

ROSA OF LIMA.   Saint Rose of Lima (Santa Rosa de Lima)
is the patron saint of Peru, and widely venerated by the
Catholic Church.   A 17th-century nun who captured widespread public notice by subjecting her flesh to mortifi-
cations, she became the first South American to be can-
onized as a saint.

ROSE, JUAN G.   Born in 1928 in Tacna.   A poet who gained
public fame by writing about social alienation.   His Obra
poética was published in 1974, his seventh book of verses.

RUIZ, BARTOLOME.   A 16th-century ship's officer and navi-

gator, Bartolomé Ruiz was born in Andalusía, Spain.
In 1526 he became chief pilot for expeditionary leader
Francisco Pizarro, exploring the coastline of southern
Colombia, Ecuador, and northern Peru.   Ruiz gathered
information from the Indians that allowed Pizarro to conquer the Inca Empire.   In 1529, Ruiz was awarded the
title "Grand Pilot of the Southern Ocean" by the Spanish
crown.

RUIZ ELDREDGE RIVERA, ALBERTO.   A politician and lawyer prominent in the 1960s and 1970s.   Alberto Ruiz
Eldredge was a founder of the Progressive Social Movement (Movimiento Social Progresista; MSP) and its 1962
presidential candidate.   From March 1970 to July 1974,
he was Peruvian Ambassador to Brazil.   In mid-1974
the government designated him executive publisher of
the expropriated daily newspaper El Expreso in Lima.

-S-

SACO MIRO QUESADA, JOSE.   Civic leader in Lima in the
1950s and 1960s.   José Saco Miró Quesada worked with
Edgardo Seoane of the Popular Action party from 1958
through 1960 on basic reforms recommended by their
Commission on Agrarian Reform and Housing.   Saco
and Seoane presented the plan to President Manuel Prado,
who never implemented it before he left office in 1962.
When Fernando Belaúnde became President in 1963, one
of his first acts was the Saco reform plan, later worked
into Law 15037, promulgated on May 21, 1964.   The
so-called "Saco Plan" began public housing projects,
some of which were later completed by the military
government of President Juan Velasco.

SAENZ, MANUELA.   Born in December 1793 in Quito.   Died
November 23, 1856, in Paita, Peru.   A heroine of the
independence movement against Spain, she saved the life
of liberator Simón Bolívar during an attempted assassination in Bogotá, Colombia.   She fled the Spaniards and
became a Peruvian resident.   Bolívar commissioned her
as a colonel in his Army of Gran Colombia, and she
wore a jacket with the insignia in her last years in Peru.

SAINTS   see   MARTIN DE PORRAS

SALA OROSCO, PEDRO.   An Air Force officer, promoted to

major general on January 1, 1965, and to lieutenant general on January 1, 1971. From 1965 to 1968, he was Director of Operations of the Peruvian Air Force. Director of Civil Aviation from January 1968 to September 1970. Minister of Labor in the cabinet of President Juan Velasco from September 1970 to July 1975. Served as President of the International Labor Organization, a United Nations affiliate, during 1974-1975.

SALAVERRY. A port city on the north-central coast of Peru, 20 kilometers south of the larger city of Trujillo and 570 kilometers north of Lima.

SALAVERRY, FELIPE SANTIAGO. Born in 1805 in Lima. In 1822, when just 17 years of age, Felipe S. Salaverry became a colonel under the command of General Antonio Sucre. At the Battle of Ayacucho in December 1824, Salaverry helped General Sucre, himself only 32 years old, defeat the last Spanish army in South America. Ten years later Salaverry authored a plan of reform through authoritarian government, advocating a strong executive dominating the legislature. In February 1835, Salaverry led troops which overthrew the liberal-supported administration of President Luis Orbegoso. A junta named young caudillo Salaverry as President of Peru before his thirtieth birthday. Soon he was driven from Lima by rival commanders and the government passed into the hands of General Agustín Gamarra and General Andrés Santa Cruz.

SALOMON-LOZANO TREATY. In 1922 Peru and Colombia signed a treaty named for the two negotiating diplomats, Salomón and Lozano, settling a boundary dispute near the Putumayo River.

SAMANEZ OCAMPO, DAVID. The elderly political leader who helped lead the Arequipa uprising which overthrew President Augusto Leguía in 1930.

SAN CARLOS, COLEGIO DE. In 1771 Toribio Rodríguez de Mendoza founded the College of San Carlos, which allowed students to study political philosophy about popular sovereignty until the Spanish crown learned about the curriculum and suppressed its courses in philosophy and natural science.

SAN JUAN, BATTLE OF. Near Chorrillos, a suburb of

present-day Lima, at the village outpost of San Juan,
Peruvian troops under Nicolás de Piérola fought Chilean
troops on January 13, 1881.   Chile won the battle and
sacked the area.

SAN LORENZO ISLAND.   The island of San Lorenzo has a
prison where dictator President Augusto B. Leguía sent
political opponents in 1921.   Ironically, in 1930, when
he was ousted from the presidency, Leguía himself was
jailed temporarily on San Lorenzo Island, before being
brought back to Callao and put into the national peniten-
tiary.

SAN MARCOS UNIVERSITY.   Peru's principal national institution of higher learning, the Universidad Nacional de
San Marcos, was founded in 1551 by a decree of Emperor
Charles V of Spain, who also authorized the National
University of Mexico in the same decree.   Ever since,
Peruvians and Mexicans have disputed which had the
first university in the New World.   By the 17th century
San Marcos had become an outstanding university with
a distinguished faculty.   During the turbulence of the
19th century San Marcos suffered periods of closure as
rival generals vied for political power.   In the 20th century, as various administrations used funds of the Ministry of Education to create other universities to teach
engineering, agriculture, technology, and the newer sciences, San Marcos lost the preeminence it enjoyed in
an earlier age when law, medicine, and philosophy were
the major curricula of universities.   As San Marcos became politicized in the 1960s, with student and faculty
groups led by Marxists, more moderate Peruvians began enrolling in the various private universities, such
as Catholic, Ricardo Palma, Pacífico, and other less
troubled provincial universities.   The reform Education
Law of 1972 greatly increased scholarships and teaching
openings for women and Indians.

SAN MARTIN.   One of the twenty-four departments of administration into which the republic is divided geographically,
the Department of San Martín is subdivided into six Provinces, one of which is the Province of San Martín.   In
the 1972 Census, the entire department contained only
162,000 inhabitants.   This department was named in
honor of General José de San Martín, a liberator of
Peru in its struggle for independence from Spain.

SAN MARTIN, JOSE DE. Born in 1778 in Yapeyú, Argentina
(Viceroyalty of La Plata). Died in 1850. Leader who
helped win independence from Spain for Peru, Argentina,
and Chile. Military and political protector of Peru during 1821 and 1822.

SAN ROMAN, MIGUEL. Born in 1802 in Puno. Minister of
War in the cabinet of President Ramón Castilla. Elected
President of Peru in 1862. Becoming gravely ill the
next year, San Román resigned as Grand Master of the
Masonic Lodge in Lima so that his priest would give
him the last rites of the Catholic Church. He died on
April 3, 1863.

SANCHEZ, LUIS ALBERTO. Born on October 12, 1900, in
Lima. Sánchez graduated from the National University
of San Marcos, where he held the chair of Peruvian and
American literature for forty years and served three
times as rector (president) of the university, during
1946-1949, 1961-1963, and 1966-1969. A leader in the
Aprista Party since its activation in Lima in 1931. Author of many books, essays, and articles in learned
journals throughout the world. His major work as a
cultural historian is the five-volume La literatura peruana, revised edition 1966. His Historia comparada de
la literatura de América, written when he was 74, has
become a standard reference since its publication in
1975.

SANCHEZ CARRION, JOSE. Born in 1787 in Lima. Died
on June 2, 1825, in Lima. The most eloquent writer
advocating a republican form of government, in the face
of opposition from the Spanish crown until 1824 and then,
during 1824-1825, from Peruvians advocating a nation-
alist Peruvian monarchy. In 1822 Sánchez Carrión published his two famous essays under the pseudonym El
solitario (The Hermit). These documents, widely reprinted in the press, crystallized the thinking of Peruvian leadership. Simón Bolívar called Sánchez Carrión
his chief Peruvian advisor.

SANCHEZ CERRO, LUIS (1890-1933). Career officer in the
infantry. Studied at several army specialized schools.
In February 1914, Sánchez Cerro led troops charging
the National Palace. Though wounded, he ousted President Guillermo Billinghurst. In August 1930, Lieutenant
Colonel Luís Sánchez Cerro began the uprising in Are-

quipa against the dictatorship of President Augusto Leguía. Hailed as a liberator upon his arrival in Lima,
Sánchez Cerro became President of Peru. Of medium
height but weighing only 120 pounds, he looked gaunt.
A mestizo or cholo of mixed Spanish-Indian-African an-
cestry, he engendered latent prejudice among aristocratic
leaders. In 1931 he ran as the presidential candidate
of the Revolutionary Union against newly-legalized APRA
candidate Víctor Haya de la Torre. Both candidates advocated assimilation of Indians into the political and social mainstream of Peru. Sánchez Cerro defeated Haya.
In 1932 Sánchez put down a civil insurrection. On April
30, 1933, he was assassinated by an Aprista.

SANTA CRUZ, ANDRES. Born in 1792 in La Paz, Bolivia
(then called Upper Peru, administratively still part of
Peru). Descended from a Spanish family paternally and
from Inca nobility maternally, Santa Cruz became a general in the independence forces fighting the Spanish. In
1827, as a spokesman for Simón Bolívar, he arranged
for Colombian troops to withdraw from Peru. On June
4, 1817, he convened a new Congress in Lima. In 1841,
Santa Cruz, living in Ecuador, was offered the presidency of Bolivia by insurgents. But rival forces pre-
vailed. Santa Cruz had to give up his ambition to become president of a proposed reunited or federated Peru
and Bolivia.

SAYAN ALVAREZ, CARLOS. A noted jurist whose writings
in the 1940s set the standard for Peruvian interpretation
of public international law. Sayán Alvarez published
Política internacional del Perú in 1943, compiling the
emergency legislation of World War II as applied to international law. He put into focus the Peruvian legal
position on neutrality, restrictions on sea vessels, asy-
lum, alien property, and enemy (Axis) submarines in
Peruvian territorial waters. His writings are on most
reading lists in Peruvian law schools.

SECHURA CONTRACT. In the coastal area of northern Peru
in the Sechura region, in 1946, newly-discovered oil re-
serves had been set aside as a national reserve. The
International Petroleum Company, a Standard Oil subsidiary, petitioned the government for a concession to
explore the region for both oil and natural gas deposits.
President José Bustamante and his Aprista political opponents both agreed that Congress should approve

the Sechura contract. Peru's two leading daily newspapers, El Comercio and La Prensa, both condemned
the proposed contract as a give-away to the IPC. La
Prensa editor Francisco Graña was killed on January 7,
1947, by two Apristas whom he had blamed for promoting the contract. Congress rejected the Sechura contract.

SEGURA GUTIERREZ, EDUARDO. Born on December 16,
1921, in Lima. Graduated from the Escuela Militar and
commissioned in the infantry in January 1946. Promoted
to brigadier general in 1972. Director of the National
Intelligence Service during 1969-1971. During 1971 a
member of the Council of Presidential Advisors (COAP).
Formulated the modernization plan for municipal government administration for President Juan Velasco. From
April 1972 to April 1974, president of the Peruvian Tel-
ephone Company. During 1974-1975, director of the
National Information Service.

SEOANE, MANUEL. Born in the 1890s in Lima. Died in
1963. Second only to founder Víctor Haya de la Torre
as a leader in the Aprista political movement. Brother
of Edgardo Seoane Corrales of the Popular Action party,
but publicly did not use the maternal family name "Corrales" after the family paternal name, as a majority of
Peruvians do to distinguish surnames, much as North
Americans utilize middle names or initials.

SEOANE CORRALES, EDGARDO. Born on May 15, 1903, in
Chorrillos, the suburban town south of Lima where the
Escuela Militar, the Army War College, and the Center
for Higher Military Studies are located. Despite spend-
ing his childhood in the very shadow of Peru's West
Point, Edgardo Seoane Corrales rejected an appointment
to the Escuela Militar and graduated from the National
Agricultural University. In 1963 he became executive
director of the National Office for Agrarian Reform Pro-
motion. Rejecting his brother's pressures to be an
Aprista leader, Edgardo helped Fernando Belaúnde establish Acción Popular in 1956. Elected Vice President
of Peru on the Popular Action ticket with Fernando Belaúnde in 1963. From 1967 to 1969, secretary general
of Acción Popular. In 1967, Seoane served as Peruvian
Ambassador to Mexico, commuting by air to Lima to
serve simultaneously as Vice President and prime minister (executive officer) of the Belaúnde cabinet. He

then served briefly as Minister of Foreign Relations,
breaking with his own administration in early 1968 to
accept the Popular Action party's nomination for president for the 1969 elections, which were never held.
Critical of President Belaúnde's oil policy, Seoane became president of the Agricultural Development Bank
under President Juan Velasco in August 1973.

SERRANO.   A person living in the Andean highlands (the
sierra) is a serrano.

SERVICIO NACIONAL DE ADIESTRAMIENTO DE INDUSTRIA
Y TURISMO.   The National Training Service of Industry
and Tourism (Servicio Nacional de Adiestramiento de Industria y Turismo; SENATI) is a government agency
teaching basic skills for probationary employees in industry, tourism, and handicraft trades.   Most SENATI
trainees have less than a ninth-grade education.

SICUANI.   A small city serving as a switching station for
the railroad running from the city of Puno northwest-
ward to the city of Cuzco.   Sicuani is located in the
southeasternmost part of the Department of Cuzco, near
the boundary of the Department of Puno and on the ancient trail which connected Cuzco to Puno during the
pre-Hispanic era of the Inca Empire.   Today an oiled,
graveled road follows that trail.   Sicuani, one-third of
the distance southward from Cuzco towards Puno, is a
trading area for Quechua Indians.

SIERRA.   The sierra, or Andean highlands, has 31 per cent
of the total land area of Peru but 53 per cent of its
total population.   The Andean Mountains cut Peru into
three geographical regions.   The coastal plain, or costa,
ranges in width from eight to 75 miles, comprising only
12 per cent of the republic's territory but containing 39
per cent of its population.   The central portion, to the
east of the costa, is the sierra, containing the tortuous
terrain of mountain peaks 18,000 to 20,000 feet above
sea-level.   East of the sierra lies the selva, or jungle
slopes, running to the Brazilian border, with 57 per cent
of the national territory but only eight per cent of Peru's
population.

SIMA.   The Industrial Service of the Navy, or Servicio Industrial de la Marina (SIMA), since 1968 has become a
growing governmental entity.   SIMA repairs both navy

and merchant marine ships, builds new vessels, manufactures machinery and parts used by the maritime entities, and coordinates marketing and distribution of steel products produced in Peru.

SINAMOS. The government in 1971 created the National System for Help for Social Mobilization, or Sistema Nacional de Apoyo a la Movilización Social (SINAMOS). With branch offices in key provincial cities, SINAMOS coordinated participation of groups of peasants and Indians in the social reform programs instituted by the military government during 1969-1978. In 1978 the government suspended SINAMOS operations.

SIP. The Inter-American Press Association, or Sociedad Interamericana de Prensa (SIP), with headquarters in Miami, Florida, represents newspaper publishers and editors of North and South America, especially in disputes with Latin American governments over expropriations and censorship. The SIP has severely criticized the government of President Juan Velasco (1968-1975) and of President Francisco Morales Bermúdez (1975-1980) for its guidance and control of Peruvian mass media. The Inter-American Broadcasters Association, or Asociación Interamericana de Radiodifusión (AIR), has made parallel protests since 1971, when the Peruvian government began buying controlling interest in all the privately-owned television stations and stock percentages for leverage control of privately-owned radio stations.

SISTEMA NACIONAL DE INFORMACION. The government's National Information System, or Sistema Nacional de Información (SINADI). Under the control of SINADI are Information Enterprise Services, or Empresas de Servicio de Información (ESI). Each ESI, in turn, produces a magazine (Perú Informa and ESI Andina), a daily news agency report (ESI Noticias), a daily radio report on government activities (Radio Perú), and a television news report (TV Perú).

SOCIALIST PARTY. The Socialist Party of Peru was first organized in 1919. Marxist philosopher José Carlos Mariátegui (1895-1930) in 1929 recruited some of the original Socialist Party members into an offshoot group. In October 1930, Luciano Castilla formally founded the Socialist Party of Peru as a Marxist group. Upon orders of the Communist International, the party then changed its name to the Communist Party of Peru (Partido Comunista del Perú; PCP).

SOCIEDAD DE AMANTES DEL PAIS. The Sociedad de Amantes del País, or Society of Devotees of the Country, on January 2, 1791, began publishing the periodical Mercurio Peruano twice a month in Lima, with most of the writers being professors at the National University of San Marcos. José Baquíjano (born in 1751 in Lima), a judge in the viceregal government, served as editor. The Society's Mercurio encouraged Spaniards born in Peru, called creoles, to challenge Spaniards born in Spain, called peninsulares, for the civic leadership of Peru. This challenge led in 1810 to the movement for independence from Spain.

SOLAR, ALEJANDRO. On April 1, 1894, the President of Peru, Remijio Morales Bermúdez (whose descendant, General Francisco Morales Bermúdez became President of Peru on August 29, 1975), died in office. A former Army colonel, Remijio Morales had been elected and inaugurated in 1890, along with a first and second vice president. According to the constitution, Morales should have been succeeded by First Vice President Alejandro Solar, a civilian. But military leaders staged a coup to oust Solar and elevated Second Vice President Justiniano Borgoño to the presidency. Borgoño, a former colonel, was loyal to the military leaders.

SOLARI SWAYNE, MANUEL. Throughout the 1960s, Manuel Solari Swayne was a widely-read and often-quoted columnist for the Lima daily newspaper, El Comercio. His recurring theme was encouragement of pride in the mestizaje, or mixed Spanish-Indian cultural heritage of Peru.

SPANISH INQUISITION. The Inquisition of the Catholic Church in Spain in 1481, which became a fanatical movement searching for heretics and, in practice, a movement of political extremists who persecuted Jews, Moslems, and even Christians suspected of not following without question the views of the Office of the Holy Brotherhood, was transplanted into Peru in 1536. When the Cortes of Cádiz in Spain abolished the Inquisition Tribunal, the government in Lima quickly suppressed its own Inquisition office. With the restoration of Ferdinand VII to the throne of Spain, the Inquisition was reestablished in both

Spain and Peru, but with the ascendancy of independence forces in Lima the office was permanently closed in 1822. In 1824, the Freemasonry movement, special target of the Inquisition office, was recognized as a legal secular philanthropic society by the new government of the Peruvian republic.

STATE OIL ENTERPRISES. Beginning with Pemex in Mexico in 1938, Latin American governments began to create government corporations for the operation of oil production: Petrovén in Venezuela, Petrobrás in Brazil, Ecopetrol in Colombia, Ancap in Uruguay, and Petroperú. The latter was created by the new military government in Lima in October 1968. Shortly thereafter, Petroperú joined the Latin American Reciprocal State Oil Producing Enterprises Association (known by its acronym in Spanish, ARPEL). ARPEL was founded on October 29, 1965, in Rio de Janeiro. The seventh ARPEL assembly was held in Lima in March 1977.

STATE SYSTEM OF PROPERTY DEVELOPMENT. In 1969, a position paper by the Council of Presidential Advisors (COAP) was entitled the "State System of Property Development." Later the plan evolved into a governmental agency called the National System of Social Property Development (Sistema Nacional de Desarrollo de la Propiedad Social; SINADEPS). In 1977, President Francisco Morales Bermúdez appointed General César Rosas Cresto as director of SINADEPS.

SUCRE, ANTONIO JOSE DE. Born February 3, 1795, in Cumaná, Venezuela. Died June 4, 1830, in Berruecos, Colombia. General Antonio José de Sucre was the national hero of the independence struggle of Ecuador, a trusted military leader of Liberator Simón Bolívar and president of the new republic of Bolivia, which in pre-independence was known as Upper Peru. In 1828, Peruvian generals encouraged opposition inside Bolivia, hoping that the fall of Sucre might help bring Upper Peru back under Peruvian sovereignty. The assassination of Sucre in Colombia in 1830 did nothing to encourage Bolivians to join Peru.

-T-

TACNA. One of the twenty-four departments of administration

into which Peru is divided geographically. It is the southernmost department and belonged to Chile during 1883-1929 as a trust area after Chile defeated Peru in the War of the Pacific. Under terms of the Treaty of Ancón of 1883, a plebiscite was to be held in ten years to determine sovereignty over Tacna. Despite the treaty provisions, Chile did not hold the specified plebiscite in 1893. Postponed again and again, the Tacna dispute between Peru and Chile resulted in a conference in Washington in 1922. In 1925, U.S. President Calvin Coolidge promised to have the United States supervise an impartial plebiscite. Instead, in 1929 Santiago and Lima leaders agreed that Tacna would belong to Peru, and Arica, the region just south of Tacna, would belong to Chile. Tacna has only two Provinces, Tacna and Tarata. In the 1972 Census, the Department of Tacna had only 66,000 inhabitants.

TAHUANTINSUYO EMPIRE. In pre-Hispanic times, Tahuantinsuyo was the Quechua name for the Inca Confederation, which became more centralized in its government as the Inca Empire. In 1532, the Inca Empire was conquered by the Spaniards.

TANGUIS, FERMIN. An agricultural scientist, Fermín Tanguis in 1912-1914 developed a better strain of Peruvian cotton, which in 1915 began to be exported, helping the republic's economy substantially.

TARAPACA, BATTLE OF. In the Battle of Tarapacá during the War of the Pacific, Peruvian forces defeated Chilean troops on November 27, 1879. But Chile later won the war.

TARAPOTO. The town of Tarapoto is midway between Peru's northern coastal ports and the city of Iquitos, deep in the Amazon jungle. Though a small town, Tarapoto maintains a large airport to accommodate refueling light planes flying between coastal towns and Iquitos.

TELLO, JULIO C. (1880-1947). The father of archaeology studies in Peruvian universities. At the National University of San Marcos, Tello encouraged seminars to stress the achievements of pre-Hispanic Indians.

TIEMPO, EL. In 1864, political leader Nicolás Piérola (acting President of Peru 1879-1881; elected constitutional

President of Peru 1895-1899) founded the daily newspaper El Tiempo in Lima to support his conservative political views.

TINGO MARIA. In the sierra, a city high in the Andes, Tingo
    María is located in the Department of Huánuco, about
    midway between the port of Chimbote on the Pacific
    coast and the Peruvian-Brazilian border in terms of
    east-west measurement, and approximately midway be-
    tween the Ecuadorian and Chilean borders in terms of
    north-south measurement. Although its 1972 Census
    population only totaled 24,000, Tingo María maintains
    an airport large enough to refuel small and medium-
    sized aircraft flying over the Andes from coastal cities
    to the eastern jungle towns. Tingo María is connected
    by land via a hard-surface road to the city of Huánuco
    to the south, and on southward to the mining region city
    of Cerro de Pasco. Thus its function as a transshipment
    point has long been vital in the Peruvian mining industry.

TITICACA, LAKE. Lake Titicaca lies partly in Peru and
    partly in Bolivia. The Peruvian city on its western
    shore, Puno, is a railroad and highway terminal to
    Peruvian cities northward and westward. The largest
    lake in South America, Titicaca measures 3,200 square
    miles in area. At an altitude of 12,508 feet above sea-
    level, Titicaca is the highest navigable lake in the world.
    Ocean-going steamships carry passengers across the
    lake on overnight trips. Indians sail their balsa-wood
    boats from village to village in various small harbors
    ringing the lake.

TOLA. A word meaning a pre-Hispanic burial place of the
    Quechua Indians.

TOLEDO, FRANCISCO DE. Toledo was Viceroy of Peru dur-
    ing 1569-1581. He conveyed the views of the Inca no-
    bility who survived the conquest of 1532, or of their
    offspring or grandchildren, back to colonial administra-
    tors in Spain, thus giving historians a reference called
    the Informaciones.

TORRE TAGLE, JOSE BERNARDO DE. Born in 1779 in
    Lima. Under the Spanish rule of the Viceroyalty of
    Peru, José Bernardo de Tagle y Portocarrero was the
    fourth Marquis of Torre Tagle. Despite his title as a
    Spanish noble, Torre Tagle on December 29, 1820, pro-

claimed independence from Spain in the northern coastal
city of Trujillo, of which he had been Spanish governor.
General José de San Martín designated Torre Tagle as
Peru's acting chief executive in 1822. In July 1823,
when Spanish forces withdrew from Lima, General Antonio Sucre proclaimed Torre Tagle interim President
of Peru. In September 1823, Torre Tagle re-invested
Simón Bolívar with the office he had held in trust.

TORRE TAGLE BALCONY. In downtown Lima, the ornate
19th-century windows and wooden and iron balcony of
the mansion which the Marquis of Torre Tagle had occupied has been preserved as a tourist attraction. The
adjacent building is part of the modern-day Ministry of
Foreign Relations.

TRANS-ANDEAN PIPELINE. The Trans-Andean Oil Pipeline,
constructed by the government's Petroperú and contracted
by Japanese companies, connects the oil fields of the
eastern Amazon jungle in northern Peru to the port of
Bayóvar on the Pacific Ocean. After full operations
began in 1977, an average 30,000 barrels a day were
being pumped from the jungle fields to the port on the
coast.

TRIBUNA, LA. A Lima daily which in 1873 urged the Peruvian government to make peace with Chile in the face of
tensions leading to the 1879 War of the Pacific. Later
the daily shut down. It was revived in the 1930s as the
voice of the Aprista political party and reached the height
of its circulation and impact in national life in 1963. In
1970, the military government of President Juan Velasco
had the courts expropriate this daily, reportedly for non-
payment of taxes, but actually to silence its criticism
of the reform laws the government had promulgated.
Instead of turning it over to a pro-government union,
as the government did with other expropriated newspapers,
a presidential decree abolished La Tribuna and sold its
printing equipment.

TRUJILLO. A city in northern Peru on the Pacific Coast,
Trujillo is located in the Department of La Libertad.
In the 1972 Census, the city of Trujillo and the sur-
rounding Province of Trujillo, which contains only the
city and a few satellite villages, had a population of
225,140. Its 1978 population was estimated at 250,000.

TUMBES. One of the twenty-four administrative departments
into which Peru is divided geographically. The Department of Tumbes is subdivided into three Provinces, one
of which is the Province of Tumbes. The 1972 Census
showed 55,812 inhabitants in the Department, and a 1978
estimate gave 67,000 as the Department's population.

TUPAC AMARU. The first Túpac Amarú was the Inca Emperor who commanded an Indian uprising put down by
Viceroy Francisco de Toledo in 1571. Túpac Amarú II
was born José Gabriel Condorcanqui, a mestizo descended
from Inca nobles and Spanish conquistadores. Infuriated
by Spanish cruelty towards Indians, Túpac Amarú II dis-
carded his Spanish nobleman attire, dressed in the traditional headdress, loincloth, and cape of the Incas,
summoned hundreds of Quechuas into a military force,
and seized a Spanish official and executed him in November 1780. Thus began an insurrection against the viceregal government, with thousands of Indians and mestizos taking up arms to fight the Spanish overlords. In
1781, Spanish troops suppressed the rebel forces and
killed the leaders.

TUPAC AMARU PLAN. The long-range plan of the military
government of President Francisco Morales Bermúdez,
giving a blueprint for continuing for the period 1977-
1985 the social and economic reforms instituted by the
military leaders since October 1968. A preliminary
draft of the Túpac Amarú Plan, named for the Indian
who fought for peasant rights in 1780, was widely circulated among civic leaders in March 1977. Then fol-
lowed months of public dialogue among military and civilian leaders, with special debates at the Center for
Higher Military Studies, and special inquiries by the
Council of Presidential Advisors (COAP). The final
version of the plan was published, with the assumption
that the civilian government to be elected in 1980 would
carry out provisions not already in effect. The plan
was officially promulgated by the government on October
9, 1977.

-U-

UCAYALI RIVER. A river arising in the eastern mountains
of Peru, the Ucayali joins the Marañón above Iquitos.

UGARTE, CESAR ANTONIO. César A. Ugarte, a prominent
    professor of economics at the National University of
    San Marcos, was enthusiastic in his praise of democracy
    as practiced in the United States. His writings encour-
    aged Peruvian scholars to try to adapt certain North
    American practices into Peruvian public life, especially
    the non-partisan aspects of the U.S. civil service merit
    system.

ULLOA, ALBERTO. Alberto Ulloa was a distinguished pro-
    fessor of international law at the National University of
    San Marcos during the 1920s and the author of some of
    Peru's foreign policies during that decade.

ULLOA, MANUEL. Minister of Finance in the cabinet of
    President Fernando Belaúnde during 1963-1968. Ulloa
    was also an official of the Deltec Banking Corporation,
    an international private development agency which was
    a major creditor of the Peruvian government in the 1960s.
    On August 9, 1968, Ulloa negotiated a large loan for
    Peru from Deltec, which the newspapers, except for
    the daily owned by Ulloa, criticized as a conflict of
    interest. When Belaúnde was ousted by the military
    on October 3, 1968, Ulloa and the other cabinet min-
    isters also lost their offices. On March 4, 1970, the
    government of President Juan Velasco had the Ministry
    of the Interior expropriate the morning daily newspaper
    El Expreso and its afternoon affiliated daily newspaper,
    La Extra, both owned by Manuel Ulloa, who was by then
    living in exile. Under the presidential decree of 1974,
    El Expreso was assigned to the Association of Workers
    in Education, which included both teachers and non-teach-
    ing employees of schools, but the government continued
    to designate the executive publisher.

UNION NACIONAL. In 1891, Manuel González Prada founded
    the National Union (Unión Nacional) political party, which
    failed to attract many members or much influence. He
    abandoned it as a small lobbying group in 1902.

UNIVERSITIES. In addition to the National University of
    San Marcos, supported directly by the national govern-
    ment, Peru has several other state-supported institutions
    in the greater metropolitan Lima area, including national
    engineering and agricultural universities, and state-fi-
    nanced universities in the major provincial cities. In
    addition, Peru has several private universities, such as

Catholic University in Lima, and Ricardo Palma and University of the Pacific.

UPPER PERU.   The vast region known during the Spanish colonial era as Upper Peru became, with the coming of independence from Spain, the republic of Bolivia, named in honor of liberator Simón Bolívar.

URETA, ELOY G.   General Eloy G. Ureta commanded the Peruvian army which defeated the troops of Ecuador at the battle of Zarmuzilla in July 1941, in a boundary dispute dating back to the early days of independence.

-V-

VALCARCEL, GUSTAVO.   Gustavo Valcárcel was the leader of the Peruvian Communist Party who led the rioters against the motorcade in downtown Lima of then U. S. Vice President Richard Nixon and his wife during a goodwill visit.   Valcárcel boasted that he threw rocks at Mr. and Mrs. Nixon and spit on members of their official party, in one of the rudest displays against a foreign dignitary ever evidenced in Peruvian history.   Valcárcel claimed he was demonstrating Peruvian impatience with foreign policies of the United States.   Some of the other Peruvians he led in the rioting, however, later expressed regrets at the vulgar and violent display, especially as Mrs. Patricia Nixon also had her life threatened, as the violence escalated before police ended the incident on May 7, 1958.

VALCARCEL, LUIS E.   Born in 1891 in Lima, Luis E. Valcárcel studied philosophy at Peruvian universities and became a writer and militant champion of Indian rights. In 1927 he published Temestad en los Andes, a book advocating violence by Indians to win more political power. In his 1945 book, Ruta cultural del Perú, Valcárcel advocated Marxist government and the destruction of white and mestizo institutions, by force if necessary.

VALCARCEL, MARIANO N.   The Civilistas' candidate for president in the election of 1894, Mariano N. Valcárcel had earlier defected from the Constitutionalist Party. Military leaders imprisoned civilian leaders, making the 1894 campaign a sham, with Valcárcel escaping from the port of Callao aboard a German ship and going into

exile in Chile. In Peru, a dishonest balloting re-elected
Andrés A. Cáceres. From 1876 to 1940, Peru's population rose steadily from 2.7 to 7 million, reaching 16
million in 1978. By 1900, only 110,000 voters were
registered out of an adult Peruvian population of 1.8
million. Valcárcel, then aged leader of the fading Civilistas, stated that Peruvians had failed to build a democracy by failing to form parties appropriate to the
adult population and said that the "activists" throughout
the republic "could fit into one railroad car."

VALDEZ ANGULO, ENRIQUE. Born on August 16, 1917, in
Arequipa. Married to Luz Marine Velasco, a cousin
of the late Peruvian President Juan Velasco. Graduated
from the Escuela Militar and commissioned in the cavalry in 1940. Attended Armor Advanced Tank Officer
Course at Fort Knox, Kentucky, 1946-1947; Escuela Su-
perior de Guerra, 1950-1951; U.S. Army Command and
Staff College at Fort Leavenworth, Kansas, 1954-1955.
Graduated from Peru's Center for Higher Military Studies (CAEM) in 1965 as a colonel. Promoted to brigadier general in 1968. Prefect of the Department of
Cuzco from October 1968 through December 1969, and
simultaneously president of the Cuzco Development and
Reconstruction Corporation. During 1970, director of
Army intelligence and director of the government's Agro-
Industrial Complexes System, from which post he ran
the agrarian reform programs. On April 1, 1971, he
became Minister of Agriculture. Upon reaching age 60
in 1977, he requested a research assignment away from
political administration.

VARGAS CABALLERO, LUIS. Born on February 10, 1916,
in Tacna. Graduated from the Escuela Naval and commissioned in December 1939. Attended the Escuela Superior de Guerra Naval in 1952. Graduated from the
Center for Higher Military Studies (CAEM) in 1963.
Promoted to rear admiral in 1968 and to vice admiral
in 1972. From January to December 1968, chief of the
Naval General Staff. From December 1968 to April
1969, Minister of Justice in the cabinet of President
Juan Velasco. Then Minister of Public Housing. In
1972, Minister of the Navy, until he resigned on May
30, 1974, protesting President Velasco's censorship of
the press. Vargas Caballero has been an outspoken
champion of freedom of the press and mass media in
general, and the recipient of awards and honors by the

Inter-American Press Association, the Inter-American
Broadcasters Association, and the press associations of
Britain, Canada, Mexico, and the Netherlands.

VARGAS LLOSA, MARIO.   Born on March 28, 1936, in Arequipa.   Attended primary school in Cochabamba, Bolivia.
Attended secondary school in Piura, Peru, graduating
from preparatory school in Lima.   Degree in literature
from the National University of San Marcos.   Completed
a doctorate in literature from the University of Madrid,
Spain.   Taught at universities in Paris, London, Barce-
lona, and the United States.   Vargas Llosa's first book
of short stories, Los jefes, won the Alas Literature
Prize in Spain in 1958.   It contained the characters
later to become well known all over Latin America in
his subsequent five major novels about social and political problems in Peru.   In 1963 the publication of La
ciudad y los perros brought him fame all over the Spanish-speaking world and, translated into English as The
Time of the Hero, brought him worldwide fame as a
novelist.   It became a best seller translated into 20
languages.   Its setting is the Prado Military Academy
in Lima, in which cadets are prototypes practicing virility rituals (machismo), political pressure, social black-
mail, and economic leverage.   His other major novels
are La casa verde in 1967, Los cachorros (The Cubs)
in 1968, Conversación en la Catedral in 1969, and Pan-
taleón in 1973, translated into English in 1977.   Entitled
Captain Pantoja and the Special Service, it was translated by Gregory Kolovakos and Ronald Christ, and published by Harper and Row.

VARGAS VICUÑA, ELODORO.   Born in 1924 in Cerro de
Pasco.   Outstanding short story writer.   His three books
have made Vargas Vicuña known throughout Peru's academic and intellectual spheres.   They are Nahuín, published in 1953; Taita Cristo, in 1964; and Zora, in 1964.

VELASCO, JUAN.   Born in 1727 in Ecuador.   Died in 1792
in Italy.   He wrote Historia del reino de Quito, the
Spanish edition of which was published in two volumes
in Quito in 1841 and 1842, and a French-language edition of which was published in Paris in 1840.   Velasco
covered the natural history, ancient history, and modern
history into the late 18th century of the lands of the
Inca Empire, from Ecuador through Peru southward into
present-day Bolivia and Chile.   He included fables as

well as factual reports, and believed that Amazon women
warriors had lived on the river named after them, and
that the fabled family tree for the Inca Emperor Atahualpa was factual. Velasco was from an aristocratic
family of Riobamba, Ecuador, and studied theology and
experimental physics at the College of San Luís. In
1744 he became a Jesuit, becoming a member of the
Corporation of Our Lady of Light. He taught literature
at San José de Popayán Academy, then traveled throughout the Viceroyalty of Peru, collecting documents from
various Spanish administrators which he used in writing
his history.

VELASCO ALVARADO, JUAN. Born on June 16, 1910, in
Piura. Died on December 24, 1977, in Lima, in a
military hospital, after his sixth operation in four years.
Attended Liceo San Miguel, then Non-commissioned Officers School at Chorrillos in 1929. As a corporal he
competed with university and preparatory school students
in a nationwide competition and won admission at the
Escuela Militar, Peru's West Point. He graduated first
in his class in 1934 and was commissioned in the Army,
a rarity then for a youth from a poor, small-town family. Attended Escuela Superior de Guerra, 1945-1946,
then the U.S. Army Caribbean Institute in the Canal
Zone. Promoted to brigadier general in 1959 and to
division general in 1965. Peru's military attaché in
France from 1962 to 1964. In 1965, Inspector General
of the Army. From 1965 to 1967, Chief of Staff of the
Army. On October 3, 1968, he led the military coup
against the government of President Fernando Belaúnde
and became President of Peru. Forced to resign the
presidency by other military leaders on August 29, 1975.
He received a state funeral with full presidential honors.

VIDAURRE, MANUEL LORENZO DE see PLAN DEL PERU

VILCABAMBA. In 1964, archaeologists rediscovered the
fabled Vilcabamba, the last haven of Inca rulers hiding
from Spanish conquerors in the 1530s. Located in the
Department of Cuzco, high in the Andes.

VILLANUEVA DEL CAMPO, ARMANDO. Secretary General
of the Aprista Party, he was reelected on July 31, 1974,
leading a slate of candidates dedicated to more militant
opposition to the military government. This was viewed
as a defeat for the party's policy of conciliation. With

the scheduling of an election of a constituent assembly
on June 18, 1978, Villanueva del Campo found renewed
rivalry among party leaders.

VILLARAN, MANUEL V.   In 1936, the new National Party
nominated for president Manuel Vicente Villarán, a longtime scholar in international law.   Incumbent Oscar R.
Benavides, serving out the unexpired term of assassinated President Luis Sánchez Cerro, cancelled the election results and arbitrarily served a full six-year term
himself.

VIVANCO, MANUEL I.   Born early in the 19th century in
Lima.   Died in 1873 in Chile.   A military leader at the
Battle of Ayachucho in December 1824; although only in
his early twenties, Vivanco commanded a force against
the Spanish troops.   He became a general before he was
thirty.   In 1873, the old general led an unsuccessful revolt against President Manuel Pardo.   Vivanco then went
into exile in Chile, dying soon after reaching Santiago.
His body was returned to Lima, where statesman Nicolás
de Piérola gave a funeral oration witnessed by hundreds.
Vivanco did not realize his ambition of being president
but did serve in 1865 as Peru's ambassador in negotiations with Spain, forcing Spain to withdraw troops from
the Chincha Islands, 100 miles offshore, southwest of
Callao.

-W-

W.   The letter "w" does not normally occur in Spanish, but
sometimes is employed in transliteration of words from
Quechua, Aymará, and other Indian languages, alternat-
ing with the Spanish "gu" and "hu," as in "huasibamba."
A few foreign words, principally from English and German, have limited use in Peru, as do a few surnames
of persons with ancestors with English, German, or other
European names.

WEISE BANK.   A longtime private banking institution founded
by a German financier who settled in Lima in the 19th
century and married into a Peruvian family.   In the
1970s the Weise corporation became a combination pri-
vate-public holding company with the reform military
government holding minority stock.

WESTPHALEN, EMILIO ADOLFO. Born in 1911 in Peru,
   the descendant of German immigrants who married into
   a Peruvian family. After publishing two volumes of
   poems, Westphalen became one of Peru's leading poets.
   Those books were Las insulas extrañas in 1933, and
   Abolición de la muerte in 1935. From 1947 to 1949,
   he edited the magazine Las Moradas, a leading literary
   journal. He was editor of the journal Amaru from 1968
   into 1971. Since 1975, Westphalen has been Peruvian
   cultural attaché in the Peruvian Embassy in Rome.

WILDER, THORNTON. American novelist and playwright, much
   revered in Peruvian circles. Although Wilder spent his
   writing career in the United States, he read, as a youth,
   the history of colonial Peru under the Spanish viceroys
   and learned of the famed Lima Theater which an actress
   maintained with the patronage of the viceroy Andrés de
   Ribeira in the 18th century. The actress, known as
   "La Perichole," was the mistress of the viceroy. The
   German-born French composer Jacques Offenbach (1819-
   1880) used the story of the viceroy and La Perichole as
   the basis for his opera "La Perichole." Thornton N.
   Wilder, born in 1897, after seeing that opera in New
   York, decided to connect it to the legends about the San
   Luis bridge which the Incas built across the Apurimac
   River in 1400. The bridge collapsed in 1880, but Wilder
   moved that event back a century to dramatize the death
   of La Perichole; the result was his novel, The Bridge
   of San Luis Rey, published in 1927 and winner of a
   Pulitzer Prize for literature. After becoming a best
   seller in English, this novel, in Spanish, became a
   classic in Peru. In 1944, it was made into a motion
   picture starring Lynn Bari, Louis Calhern, Akim Tam-
   iroff, and Francis Lederer.

WILSON AVENUE. One of the main streets running southward
   from downtown Lima, Avenida Wilson, named in honor
   of U.S. president Woodrow Wilson, extends from Avenida Uruguay due south to Avenida 28 de Julio, a principal artery for buses and automobiles headed for the suburbs of Lince, San Isidro, and Miraflores. The northern half of Wilson Avenue has been renamed for the Inca
   leader Garcilaso de la Vega, but in the late 1970s Peruvians were calling the thoroughfare by both names.

WORLD WAR TWO. Peru broke diplomatic relations with the
   Axis (Germany, Italy, and Japan) in 1942 and began

rounding up Nazi and Fascist spies. Also in 1942, Peru declared war on the Axis, becoming officially one of the allies of the United States, and hence, a charter founding member of the United Nations in 1945 in San Francisco.

-X-

XAVIER INSTITUTE. The Instituto San Xavier, launched by Jesuit priests in 1950, attempted to create a Christian Democratic think-tank similar to the Rand Corporation in Santa Monica, California, but by 1958 had run out of funds and participants.

XIMENA, RAFAEL. Born in 1789 in Guayaquil, Ecuador. Died on April 11, 1830, in Lima. An army colonel who helped Ecuador win its independence from Spain, Ximena pushed Ecuador's independence from the Gran Colombia federation of Venezuela, Colombia, and Ecuador. Moving to Lima, Ximena became a Peruvian citizen and held several key positions in the Peruvian government between 1827 and his passing in 1830.

-Y-

YANACONA. In the 19th century, a yanacona was an Indian who had been a servant of the Spaniards before colonialism ended in the 1820s.

YDIAGUES, JOSE DE. A prominent 19th-century expert on Peruvian commercial law. His most noted work was Legislación peruana relativa a concesiones de patentes de privilegio, published in 1878. It was the pioneer definitive work on royalties from inventions patented in Peru, and was the basis for the 1945 modernized version of Peruvian patent law. There is a Ydiagues collection in the leading Lima law libraries.

YOUNG TOWNS. The "pueblos jóvenes" or "young towns" are the new slums which have mushroomed on the edges of the industrial regions of the greater Lima metropolitan area. The government's National Mobilization Service (SINAMOS) has a special office to deal with the problems of the young town hovels, shacks, and unsanitary crowded living conditions. Funds from the United States have been channeled through the Agency for International Development. From the late 1960s through the 1970s the U.S. Embassy in Lima had a full-time staff officer from AID assigned to work with SINAMOS on the young town problems and similar projects.

YOUTH OF CUZCO. In 1930 in Cuzco, a new political group called the Juventud del Cuzco (Youth of Cuzco) was formed to give public support to new President Luis Sánchez Cerro, the 40-year-old lieutenant colonel who had just overthrown the eleven-year dictatorship of Augusto Leguía. The Cuzco group was the most articulate of several similar regional groups advocating basic social reforms, some of which were not carried out until the military reformers under General Juan Velasco finally took power in October 1968, some 38 years later.

YUNGAY, BATTLE OF. On January 20, 1839, at Yungay, high in the Andes north of Lima, the Battle of Yungay was the confrontation between the forces of a confederation led by Chilean General Manuel Bulnes and Peruvian General Agustín Gamarra on the one hand, and the forces led by Bolivian General Andrés Santa Cruz and Peruvian General Luis Orbegoso in a rival confederation with Bolivian troops. The latter lost and Santa Cruz went into exile.

-Z-

ZARUMILLA, BATTLE OF. In July 1941, Ecuador asserted territorial claims along its southwestern boundary with Peru in the region of the town of Zarumilla. Ecuadorian troops launched an undeclared war. General Eloy Ureta led a victorious Peruvian army in the Battle of Zarumilla. Peace negotiations in 1942 at Rio de Janeiro, under the auspices of Argentina, Brazil, Chile, and the United States, established Peruvian sovereignty over the region.

ZAVALETA, CARLOS EDUARDO. Born on March 7, 1928, in the town of Caraz in the Department of Ancash, Peru. Graduated from the National University of San Marcos in 1958. His doctoral dissertation on U.S. novelist William Faulkner won the González Prada National Prize for literary criticism in 1959. Zavaleta translated and interpreted into Peruvian cultural terms the writings of Nathaniel Hawthorne and James Joyce. Zavaleta did

graduate work at universities in the United States and
in Spain, and at the University of London. After teaching English and Spanish literature at Peruvian universities, he has been, since 1965, a professional diplomat as cultural attaché at Peruvian embassies in La
Paz, Mexico City, and Madrid. In his 1974 book Los
apréndices, Zavaleta captures the customs of the Andean
villages in which he spent the first 14 years of his childhood.

ZAVALETA CRUZADO, ROGER. Professor of law at the
University of Trujillo, the important provincial university in the northern coastal city of Trujillo. In 1963
and 1969 he published volumes on Peruvian civil procedure which are generally considered to be definitive,
and which in the 1970s have been used as standard law
school textbooks throughout Peru.

ZILERI GIBSON, ENRIQUE. Editor of Peru's leading news
magazine, Caretas. After the military government came
to power in October 1968, Zileri began to be a major
target of censors as his skilled and satirical pen pointed
out inconsistencies in bureaucratic verbiage and the
abridgment of political rights in the name of a social revolution. In June 1974, Caretas was closed down for
having an "anti-revolutionary attitude, displayed by criticizing the government." Zileri was deported. When
General Francisco Morales Bermúdez replaced General
Juan Velasco Alvarado as President of Peru on August
29, 1975, one of the first big changes was an easing of
pressures on the mass media. On September 2, 1975,
Morales nullified by decree the orders of Velasco, who
a few weeks before had exiled several journalists critical of the government. Enrique Zileri returned from
exile and by mid-1977 had his magazine back to its
former high professional level. News stand copies
would be sold out within two days after each issue
came out.

ZIMMERMAN ZAVALA, AUGUSTO. For many years, Zimmerman Zavala was editor of the Lima daily newspaper,
El Comercio. Late in 1968 he resigned from the newspaper to become head of the Oficina Nacional de Información, with an office in the Presidential Palace.

ZUÑIGA, CARLOS IVAN. A prominent commentator in the
field of criminal law in the 1960s, Zúñiga in 1957 pub-

lished <u>La teoría jurídica del homicidio</u>, which explained the treatment of murder cases under Peru's penal code.

ZURRON. A leather sack for packing cocoa beans before they are sent to market. A zurrón is also the larger container holding four smaller sacks, ready for crating for export in the holds of merchant ships. In Andean villages, Peruvian Indians use the word "zurron" to mean a shepherd's pouch, which always contains the wooden flute used to charm and lead llamas up and down the mountain trails.

ZUTANO. A zutano in Peru is a John Doe, the average citizen.

APPENDICES

Appendix A

CHRONOLOGY OF RULERS OF THE INCA EMPIRE

In pre-Hispanic times, Incas ruled the Peruvian Empire from 1021 A.D., when Mancocapac I began his forty-year reign. From 1062 A.D. until the arrival of the Spaniards in 1532, thirteen other Incas ruled an empire stretching from present-day northern Chile and Bolivia to Ecuador. Included was one female monarch, Yaguar Guacac, who reigned from 1249 to 1289 A.D. and then resigned her office, ceding her crown to her son, Viracocha, who ruled into 1340 A.D., or fifty-one years, the second longest reign of any Inca emperor. The longest rule was that of Pachacutec, sixty years.

Name	Dates of Reign (A.D.)	Years of Rule
Inca Urco	1340	11 days
Pachacutec	1340 to 1400	60 years
Yupanqui	1400 to 1439	39 years
Túpac Yupanqui	1439 to 1475	36 years
Huayna Capac	1475 to 1525	50 years
Huáscar	1526 to 1532	7 years
Atajualpa	1532 to 1533	14 months

(Puppet rulers under the Spaniards)

Manco Capac	1535 to 1555	20 years
Sayri Túpac	1553 to 1559	7 years
Cusitito Yupanqui	1563 to 1569	6 years
Túpac Amarú	1569 to 1571	3 years

After 1571, the Spanish Viceroys made no pretense of

119

maintaining puppet Indian emperors for the former Inca Empire, which by then was completely reorganized as the Viceroyalty of Peru of the Spanish Empire.

Appendix B

DEPARTMENTS OF THE REPUBLIC OF PERU

The 24 Departments of the Republic of Peru, with the subdivisional Provinces within each Department, are:

AMAZONAS: Bagua, Bongará, Chachapoyas, Luya, Rodríguez de Mendoza.

ANCASH: Aija, Bolognesi, Carhuaz, Casma, Corongo, Huaraz, Huari, Huaylas, Mariscal Luzuriaga, Pallasca, Pomabamba, Recuay, Raymondi, Santa, Siguas, Yungay.

APURIMAC: Abancay, Aimaraes, Andahuaylas, Antabamba, Cotabambas, Grau.

AREQUIPA: Arequipa, Caylloma, Camaná, Caraveli, Castilla, Condesuyos, Islay, La Unión.

AYACUCHO: Cangallo, Huamanga, Huanta, La Mar, Lucanas, Parinacochas, Víctor Fajardo.

CAJAMARCA: Cajabamba, Cajamarca, Celedín, Chota, Contumaza, Cutervo, Hualgayoc, Jaén, San Ignacio, San Miguel, Santa Cruz.

CALLAO: A Province with the constitutional status of a Department.

CUZCO: Acomayo, Anta, Calca, Canas, Canchis, Chumbivilcas, Cuzco, Espinar, La Convención, Paruro, Paucartambo, Quispicanchis, Urubamba.

HUANCAVELICA: Acombaba, Angaraes, Castrovirreyna, Huancavélica, Tayacajá.

HUANUCO: Ambo, Dos de Mayo, Huamalies, Huánuco, Leoncio Prado, Marañón, Pachitea.

121

ICA: Chincha, Icá, Nazca, Palpa, Pisco.

JUNIN: Concepción, Huancayo, Jauja, Junín, Satipo, Tarma, Yauli.

LA LIBERTAD: Bolívar, Huamachuco, Otuzco, Pacasmayo, Pataz, Santiago de Chuco, Trujillo.

LAMBAYEQUE: Chiclayo, Ferreñafe, Lambayeque.

LIMA: Cajatambo, Cañete, Canta, Chancay, Huarochiri, Lima, Yauyos.

LORETO: Alto Amazonas, Coronel Portillo, Loreto, Maynas, Requena, Ucayali.

MADRE DE DIOS: Manu, Tahuamanu, Tambopata.

MOQUEGUA: General Sánchez Cerro, Mariscal Nieto.

PASCO: Daniel Carrión, Oxapampa, Pasco.

PIURA: Ayabaca, Huancabamba, Morropón, Paita, Piura, Sullana, Talra.

PUNO: Azángaro, Carbaya, Chucuito, Huancané, Lampa, Melgar, Puno, Sandia, San Román.

SAN MARTIN: Huallaga, Lamas, Mariscal Cáceres, Moyobamba, Rioja, San Martín.

TACNA: Tacna, Tarata.

TUMBES: Contraalmirante Villar, Tumbes, Zarumilla.

Appendix C

INITIALS AND ACRONYMS FOR
PARTIES AND INSTITUTIONS

AP   Acción Popular, or Popular Ac-
                      tion (political party).

APRA   Alianza Popular Revolucionaria
                      Americana, or American Popu-
                      lar Revolucionary Alliance.

CADE   Conferencia Anual de Ejecutivos,
                      or Annual Conference of Execu-
                      tives.

CAEM   Centro de Altos Estudios Mili-
                      tares, or Center for Higher
                      Military Studies.

CGTP   Confederación General de Traba-
                      jadores del Perú, or General
                      Federation of Workers of Peru,
                      or Peruvian General Federation
                      of Labor.

COAP   Comité de Asesoramiento a la
                      Presidencia, or Committee of
                      Presidential Advisors, or Coun-
                      cil of Advisement of the Presi-
                      dency.

CTP   Confederación de Trabajadores
                      del Perú, or Federation of Work-
                      ers of Peru, or Peruvian Fed-
                      eration of Labor.

CTRP   Confederación de Trabajadores
                      de la Revolución Peruana, or

Federation of Workers of the
Peruvian Revolution.

ECHAP

Empresa de Comercio de Harina
de Pesca, or Fish Meal Commerce Enterprise.

EPCHAP

Empresa Pública de Comercio
de Marina de Pesca, or Public
Fish Meal Commerce Enterprise,
an earlier version of EPCHAP.

EPSEP

Empresa Pública de Servicios
de Pesca, or Public Fish Products Services Enterprise.

FD

Frente Democrática, or Democratic Front, political alliance
of 1933.

FEP

Federación Estudantil Peruana,
or Peruvian Student Federation.

GAC

Guano Administrative Company,
incorporated in Lima in English,
not Spanish, by President Augusto Leguía, as a government
entity in 1920.

IPC

International Petroleum Company,
a subsidiary of Standard Oil of
New Jersey.

JAP

Juventud Aprista Peruana, or
Peruvian Aprista Youth.

LAFTA

Latin American Free Trade Association.

MIR

Movimiento de la Izquierda Revolucionaria, or Movement of the
Revolutionary Left.

ONDEPJOV

Organización Nacional de los
Pueblos Jóvenes, or National
Organization for Development of
the Young Towns (which are the

slums or shanty towns in metropolitan areas).

PAP   Partido Aprista Peruano, or the
Peruvian Aprista Party (newer
name for the APRA).

PCP   Partido Comunista Peruano, or
Peruvian Communist Party.

PDC   Partido Demócrata Cristiano, or
Christian Democratic Party.

PDRP   Partido Democrático Reformista
Peruano, or Peruvian Democratic
Reformist Party (legalized in
1977).

PMDP   Partido del Movimiento Democrático Peruano, or Peruvian
Democratic Movement Party.

PSR   Partido Socialista Revolucionario,
or Revolutionary Socialist Party.

RN   Radio Nacional, or National Radio (government network).

SENATI   Servicio Nacional de Adiestramiento de Industria y Turismo,
or National Training Service of
Industry and Tourism.

SINADI   Sistema Nacional de Información,
or National System of Informa-
tion (government public relations
agency).

SINAMOS   Sistema Nacional de Apoyo a la
Movilización Social, or National
System of Support for Social
Mobilization.

SIP   Sociedad Interamericana de
Prensa, or Inter-American Press
Association.

SISNADEPS or SINADEPS	Sistema Nacional de Desarrollo de la Propiedad Social, or National System of Social Property Development.
UE	Unidades Escolares, or School Building Complexes (educational plants housing both primary and secondary schools adjacent to each other).
UN	Unión Nacional, or National Union, a political party, 1881-1902.
UNO	Unión Nacional Odriísta, or Odriísta National Union, a political party from 1962 to 1968, revived in 1977 as Unión Nacional but retaining the initials "UNO" for the 1978 election ballot.

Appendix D

RECENT PRESIDENTS OF PERU

President	Years in Office
General Manuel Odría	October 1948-July 1956
Manuel Prado	July 1956-July 1962
General Ricardo Pérez Godoy	July 1962-March 1963
General Nicolás Lindley López	March 1963-July 1963
Fernando Belaúnde Terry	July 28, 1963-October 3, 1968
General Juan Velasco Alvarado	October 3, 1968-August 29, 1975
General Francisco Morales Bermúdez	August 29, 1975-1980 (presumed)

Elections

June 10, 1962	Votes	Percentage
Haya de la Torre of APRA	557,047	32.98
Belaúnde of Popular Action	544,180	32.10
Odría of UNO	480,798	28.45
Four minor candidates	108,593	6.47

Constitution requires 33.3 per cent of votes for direct election.

June 9, 1963

	Votes	Percentage
Belaúnde of Popular Action	708,000	39.0

127

Haya de la Torre of		
APRA	623,000	34.3
Odría of UNO	463,000	25.5

June 18, 1978

Seats for a Constituent Assembly.

Forthcoming in 1980

Election of a President and a Congress (Diputados and Senadores).

Appendix E

MEMBERSHIP IN CONSTITUENT ASSEMBLY
(100 Seats Elected in June 1978; Convened July 28, 1978)

Partido Aprista Peruano
(APRA), 37 members:

Victor Raúl Haya de la Torre
Luis Alberto Sánchez
Ramiro Prialé Prialé
Pedro Arana Quiroz
Andrés Townsend Ezcurra
Carlos Enrique Melgar López
Mario Peláez Bazán
Humberto Carranza Piedra
Arturo Miranda Valenzuela
Jorge Lozada Stambury
Jorge Torres Vallejo
César Vizcarra Vargas
Luis Heysen Incháustegui
Gustavo García Mundaca
Luis Rivera Tamayo
Luis Negreiros Criado
Josmel Muñoz Córdova
Eulogio Tapia Olarte
Carlos Rocca Cáceres
Javier Valle Riestra Gonzales
Fernando León de Vivero
Saturnino Berrospi Méndez
Luis Rodriguez Vildósola
Alfonso Ramos Alva
Guillermo Baca Aguinaga
Lucio Muñiz Flores
Lucio Galarza Villar
Arnaldo Alvarado Degrégori
Alan García Pérez
Carlos Manuel Cox Roose
Enrique Chirinos Soto
Carlos Enrique Ferreyros

Francisco Chirinos Soto
Julio Cruzado Zavala
Romualdo Biaggi Rodríguez
Urbino Julve Ciriaco
Héctor Vargas Haya

Partido Popular Cristiano
(PPC), 25 members:

Luis Bedoya Reyes
Rafael Vega García
Mario Polar Ugarteche
Manuel Kawashita Nagano
Ernesto Alayza Grundy
Roberto Ramírez del Villar
Clohaldo Salazar Peñalillo
Miguel Angel Mufarech
Moisés Woll Dávila
Lauro Muñoz Garay
Oscar Olivares Montano
Miguel Angel Arévalo del
  Valle
Celso Sotomarino Chávez
Gabriela Porto Cárdenas de
  Power
Jorge Neyra Bisso
Edwin Montesinos Ruiz
Rafael Risco Boado
Federico Tovar Freyre
Rubén Chang Gamarra
Xavier Barrón Cabreros
Pedro Gotuzzo Fernandini
Alberto Thorndike Elmore
Armando Buendía Gutiérrez
Génix Ruiz Hidalgo

129

Andrés Aramburú Menchaca

Frente Obrero Campesino Estudantil y Popular (FOCEP), 12 members:

Hugo Blanco Galdós
Genaro Ledesma Izquieta
Hernán Cuentas Anci
Saturnino Paredes Macedo
Romaín Ovidio Montoya Chávez
Juan Cornejo Gómez
Ricardo Napurí Schapiro
Victoriano Lázaro Gutiérrez
Germán Chamba Calle
Enrique Fernández Chacón
Magda Benavides Morales
César Augusto Mateu Moya

Partido Comunista Peruano (PCP), 6 members:

Jorge del Prado Chávez
Alejandro Olivera Vila
Isidoro Gamarra Ramírez
Raúl Acosta Salas
Eduardo Castillo Sánchez
Luis Alberto Delgado Béjar

Partido Socialista Revolucionario (PSR), 6 members:

Leonidas Rodríguez Figueroa
Avelino Mar Arias
Antonio Meza Cuadra
Miguel Echeandía Urbina

Alberto Ruiz Eldredge Rivera
Antonio Aragón Gallegos

Unidad Democrático-Popular (UDP), 4 members:

Victor Cuadros Paredes
Javier Diez Canseco Cisneros
Ricardo Díaz Chávez
Carlos Malpica Silva Santisteban

Frente Nacional de Trabajadores y Campesinos (FNTC), 4 members:

Roger Cáceres Velásquez
Pedro Cáceres Velásquez
Ernesto Sánchez Fajardo
Jesús Véliz Lizárraga

Partido Demócrata Cristiano (PDC), 2 members:

Héctor Cornejo Chávez
Carlos Arturo Moretti Ricardi

Movimiento Democrático Peruano (MDP), 2 members:

Marco Antonio Garrido Malo
Javier Ortiz de Zevallos

Unión Nacional (UNO), 2 members:

Víctor Freundt Rosell
Manuel Adrianzén Castillo

BIBLIOGRAPHY

CONTENTS OF BIBLIOGRAPHY

BIBLIOGRAPHY

1. General Introduction to Peru

American University, Foreign Area Studies Division. Area Handbook for Peru. Washington, D. C. : Government Printing Office, 1972.

Basadre, Jorge. Historia de la República del Perú, 5th ed. Lima: Historia, 1961.

Bourricaud, Francois. Power and Society in Contemporary Peru. New York: Praeger, 1970.

Chaplin, David, ed. Peruvian Nationalism: A Corporatist Revolution. New Brunswick, N. J. : Transaction Books, 1976.

Delgado, Carlos. Problemas sociales en el Perú contemporáneo. Lima: Instituto de Estudios Peruanos, Series No. 6, 1971.

Martínez de la Torre, Ricardo. Apuntes para una interpretación marxista de historia social del Perú. Lima: Empresa Editorial Peruana, 1947.

Matos Mar, José, et al. Peru, hoy. México, D. F. : Siglo XXI, 1971.

2. Anthropological Introduction

Adams, Richard N. A Community in the Andes: Muquiyauyo. Seattle: University of Washington Press, 1959.

Doughty, Paul L. Huaylas: An Andean District in Search of Progress. Ithaca, N. Y. : Cornell University Press, 1968.

133

Gibson, Charles. The Inca Concept of Sovereignty and the
    Spanish Administration in Peru. Austin: University of
    Texas Institute of Latin American Studies, 1948.

Holmberg, Allan R. , et al. Vicos: método y práctica de
    antropología aplicada. Lima: Editorial Estudios Andinos,
    1966.

Patch, Richard. Periodic reports on Peru, American Univer-
    sity Field Staff. West Coast of South America Series.
    New York: 1960-1972.

3. Political System

a) In General

Alisky, Marvin. "Peru," in Ben G. Burnett and Kenneth F.
    Johnson, eds. , Political Forces in Latin America.
    Belmont, California: Wadsworth Publishing, 1968;
    2nd edition, 1970.

_____. Peruvian Political Perspective. Tempe: Center
    for Latin American Studies, Arizona State University,
    1972; 2nd edition, 1975.

Astiz, Carlos. Pressure Groups and Power Elites in Peru-
    vian Politics. Ithaca, N. Y. : Cornell University Press,
    1969.

Chaplin, David. "Peru's Postponed Revolution," World Pol-
    itics, April 1968, pp. 393-420.

_____. "Peruvian Social Mobility," Journal of Inter-Amer-
    ican Studies, October 1968, pp. 547-570.

Colter, Julio. "Crisis política y populismo militar en el
    Perú," Revista Mexican de Sociología, April-June 1970,
    pp. 737-784.

Cornejo Chávez, Héctor. Qué se propone la Democracia
    Cristiana. Lima, Perú: Ediciones del Sol, 1962.

De Las Casas, Pedro; De Las Casas, Angel, and Llosa, Au-
    gusto. Análisis de la participación de la comunidad in-
    dustrial en el capital social de la empresa. Lima,
    Perú: Universidad del Pacifico, 1970.

Delgado Olivera, Carlos. Testimonio de lucha. Lima, Peru: Editorial Peisa, 1973.

DeProspro, Ernest R. , Jr. "The Administration of the Peruvian Land Reform. " Doctoral dissertation, unpublished, Pennsylvania State University, 1967.

Dew, Edward. Politics in the Altiplano: The Dynamics of Change in Rural Peru. Austin: University of Texas Press, 1969.

Dickerson, Mark O. "Peru's Experiment in 'Revolution': the Quest for a Model. " Paper presented at the meeting of the Canadian Political Science Association at Fredericton, New Brunswick, on June 11, 1977.

Dobyns, Henry F. , and Vásquez, Mario C. , eds. Migración e integración en el Perú. Lima, Perú: Editorial Estudios Andinos, Monografías Andinas No. 2, 1963.

Epstein, Edward. "Multinational Bases for Loyalty in the Peruvian Aprista Party. " Doctoral dissertation, unpublished, University of Illinois, 1972.

Epstein, Erwin H. "Education and Peruanidad: 'Internal' Colonialism in the Peruvian Highlands," Comparative Education Review, June 1971, pp. 188-201.

Fishel, John T. "Politics and Progress in the Peruvian Sierra: a Comparative Study of Development in Two Districts. " Doctoral dissertation, unpublished, Indiana University, 1971.

Forrester, Virginia O'Grady. "Christian Democracy in Peru. " Doctoral dissertation, unpublished, Columbia University, 1970.

Gall, Norman. "Peru: the Master Is Dead," Dissent, June 1971, pp. 281-320.

Gitlitz, John S. "Impressions of the Peruvian Agrarian Reform," Journal of Inter-American Studies, July-October 1971, pp. 456-474.

Goodsell, Charles T. "That Confounding Revolution in Peru," Current History, January 1975, pp. 20-23.

Grayson, George W. "Peru's Revolutionary Government,"
    Current History, February 1973, pp. 61-63, 87.

Hilliker, Grant. The Politics of Reform in Peru. Baltimore:
    Johns Hopkins Press, 1971.

Jaquette, Jane S. "The Politics of Development in Peru."
    Ithaca, N.Y. : Mimeographed Dissertation Series, Latin
    American Studies, Cornell University, 1971.

Ledesma, A. J. "A Tree Grows in Peru," America, June
    22, 1974, pp. 28-29.

Lockhart, James. The Men of Cajamarca. Austin: Univer-
    sity of Texas Press, 1972.

Loeb, J. I. "Irony in Peru: Expropriation of the Cerro
    Corporation," New Republic, February 9, 1974, pp. 8-9.

Lowenthal, Abraham F. "Peru's Ambitious Revolution," For-
    eign Affairs, July 1974, pp. 799-817.

_____, ed. The Peruvian Experiment: Continuity and
    Change Under Military Rule. Princeton, N.J. : Prince-
    ton University Press, 1975.

Malloy, James M. "Authoritarianism, Corporatism, and Mo-
    bilization in Peru," Review of Politics, January 1974,
    pp. 52-84.

_____. "Dissecting the Peruvian Military: Review Essay,"
    Journal of Inter-American Studies and World Affairs,
    August 1973, pp. 375-382.

_____. "Populismo militar en el Perú y Bolivia," Estu-
    dios Andinos, Vol. 2, No. 2, 1971-72, pp. 113-136.

Milenky, Edward S. "Developmental Nationalism in Practice,"
    Inter-American Economic Affairs, Vol. 26, No. 4,
    1973, pp. 49-68.

Quijano Obregón, Aníbal. "Tendencia in Peruvian Develop-
    ment and in the Class Structure," in Latin America:
    Reform or Revolution? Greenwich, Connecticut: Faw-
    cett Publications, 1968.

Rozman, S. L. "The Revolution of the Political Role of the

Peruvian Military," Journal of Inter-American Studies, October 1970, pp. 539-564.

Stephens, Richard H. Wealth and Power in Peru. Metuchen, N. J. : Scarecrow Press, 1971.

Strasma, John. "The United States and Agrarian Reform in Peru," in Daniel A. Sharp, ed. , U.S. Foreign Policy and Peru. Austin: University of Texas Press, 1973.

Tullis, F. LaMond. Lord and Peasant in Peru: A Paradigm of Political and Social Change. Cambridge, Mass. : Harvard University Press, 1970.

Vandendries, René. "An Appraisal of the Reformist Development Strategy of Peru," in Robert E. Scott, ed. , Latin American Modernization Problems. Urbana: University of Illinois Press, 1973.

b) Leaders and Groups

Alba, Victor. Peru. Boulder, Col. : Westview Press, 1977.

Alexander, Robert J. , ed. Aprismo: The Ideas and Doctrines of Victor Raúl Haya de la Torre. Kent, Ohio: Kent State University Press, 1973.

Bono, A. A. "Peru: Creeping at a Petty Pace," Commonweal, February 15, 1974, pp. 467-477.

Bourricaud, Francois. La oligarquía en el Perú. Lima: Instituto de Estudios Peruanos, 1969.

Collier, David. Squatters and Oligarchs: Modernization and Public Policy in Peru. Baltimore: Johns Hopkins Press, 1977.

Colter, Julio. "Traditional Haciendas and Communities in a Context of Political Mobilization in Peru" in Rodolfo Stavenhagen, ed. , Agrarian Problems and Peasant Movements in Latin America. New York: Anchor Books, 1970.

_____, and Portocarrero, Felipe. "Peru: Peasant Organizations," in Henry Landsberger, ed. , Latin American Peasant Movements. Ithaca, N. Y. : Cornell University Press, 1969.

Bibliography   138

Craig, Wesley. "The Peasant Movement of La Convención,"
    in Henry Landsberger, ed. , Latin American Peasant
    Movements. Ithaca, N. Y. : Cornell University Press,
    1969.

Delgado, Carlos. Problemas sociales en el Perú contempor-
    aneo. Lima: Instituto de Estudios Peruanos, 1971.

_____. Testimonio de lucha. Lima: Editorial Peisa,
    1973.

Dietz, Henry A. "The Office and the Poblador: Perceptions
    and Manipulations of Housing Authorities by the Lima
    Urban Poor. " Unpublished paper at the meeting of the
    American Society for Public Administration, Los Angeles,
    California, April 1973.

_____. "Urban Squatter Settlements in Peru," Journal of
    Inter-American Studies, July 1969, pp. 353-370.

Ferrero, Rómulo. "Economic Development of Peru," in Com-
    mittee for Economic Development, ed. , Economic De-
    velopment Issues: Latin America. New York: CED
    Supplementary Paper No. 21, 1967.

Fitchett, Delbert. "Agricultural Land Tenure Arrangements
    on the Northern Coast of Peru," Inter-American Eco-
    nomic Affairs, Summer 1965, pp. 65-86.

Gómez, Rudolph. The Peruvian Administrative System. Boul-
    der, Col. : University of Colorado Bureau of Govern-
    mental Research, 1969.

Goodwin, Richard. "Letter from Peru," New Yorker, May
    17, 1969, pp. 41-109.

Hopkins, Jack W. The Government Executive of Modern Peru.
    Gainesville, Fla. : University of Florida Center for Latin
    American Studies, 1967.

Kantor, Harry. The Ideology and Program of the Peruvian
    Aprista Movement. Washington, D. C. : Savile Books,
    1966.

Kilty, Dan R. Planning for Development in Peru. New York:
    Praeger, 1967.

Lewis, Robert A. Employment, Income and the Growth of
    the Barriada in Lima, Peru. Ithaca, N.Y.: Cornell
    University Latin American Studies Dissertation Series,
    1973.

McCoy, Terry L. "Congress, the President, and Political
    Instability in Peru," in Weston Agor, ed., Latin Amer-
    ican Legislatures. New York: Praeger, 1971.

Marett, Robert. Peru. New York: Praeger, 1969.

Matos Mar, José, et al. El Perú actual. México, D. F.:
    Universidad Nacional Autónoma de México Instituto de
    Investigaciones Sociales, 1970.

Neira, Hugo. El golpe de estado: Perú 1968. Madrid,
    Spain: Editorial XYZ, 1969.

Paulston, Rolland G. Society, Schools, and Progress in Peru.
    Oxford, England: Pergamon Press, 1971.

Payne, James. Labor and Politics in Peru. New Haven:
    Yale University Press, 1965.

Pringle, J. "Peru's Leftwing Junta," Newsweek, April 8,
    1974, p. 40.

Robin, John P. and Terzo, Frederick C. Urbanization in
    Peru. New York: The Ford Foundation, 1970.

Roemer, Michael. Fishing for Growth: Export-led Develop-
    ment in Peru, 1950-67. Cambridge: Harvard Univer-
    sity Press, 1970.

Tullis, F. LaMond. Lord and Peasant in Peru. Cambridge:
    Harvard University Press, 1970.

Villanueva, Víctor. El militarismo en el Perú. Lima: Em-
    presa Gráfica Scheuch, 1962.

Webb, Richard. "Government Policy and the Distribution of
    Income in Peru, 1963-73," Research Program in Eco-
    nomic Development, Woodrow Wilson School, Princeton
    University, Paper No. 39, 1973.

Wils, Frits. Industry and Industrialists in the Metropolitan

Area of Lima-Callao, Peru. The Hague, Netherlands: Institute of Social Studies, 1970.

c) Special Political Entities and Concepts

Alisky, Marvin. "Peru's SINAMOS: Governmental Agency for Coordinating Reforms," Public Affairs Bulletin (ASU Institute of Public Administration), Vol. 11, No. 1, 1972, pp. 1-4.

Astiz, Carlos A. "The Military Establishment as a Political Elite: The Peruvian Case," in David H. Pollack and Arch R. Ritter, eds., Latin American Prospects for the 1970's: What Kinds of Revolutions? New York: Praeger, 1973.

Baines, John M. Revolution in Peru: Mariátegui and the Myth. Tuscaloosa: University of Alabama Press, 1972.

Belaúnde, Fernando. Peru's Own Conquest. Lima: American Studies Press, 1965.

_____. La realidad nacional, 3rd ed. Lima: Ediciones Mercurio Peruano, 1963.

Blanco, Hugo. Land or Death: the Peasant Struggle in Peru. New York: Pathfinder Press, 1972.

Bourque, Susan C. Cholification and the Campesino: a Study of Three Peruvian Peasant Organizations in the Process of Social Change. Ithaca, N.Y.: Cornell University Latin American Studies Dissertation Series, 1971.

_____. "El sistema político peruano y las organizaciones campesinas," Estudios Andinos (Instituto Boliviano, La Paz), Vol. II, No. 1, 1971, pp. 37-60.

Chaplin, David. The Peruvian Industrial Labor Force. Princeton, N.J.: Princeton University Press, 1967.

Clinton, Richard L. "APRA: an Appraisal," Journal of Inter-American Studies, April 1970, pp. 280-297.

Cornejo Chávez, Héctor. Qué se propone la Democracia Cristiana. Lima: Ediciones del Sol, 1962.

141 Bibliography

Doughty, Paul L. "Community Response to Natural Disaster in the Peruvian Andes." Unpublished paper at the meeting of the American Anthropological Association, New York City, September 1971.

Einaudi, Luigi R. "The Military and Government in Peru," in Clarence E. Thurber and Lawrence S. Graham, eds., Development Administration in Latin America. Durham, N.C.: Duke University Press, 1973.

_____. The Peruvian Military: a Summary Political Analysis. Memo RM-6048-RC. Santa Monica, Cal.: The Rand Corporation, May 1969.

_____. "Revolution from Within--Military Rule in Peru Since 1968," Studies in Comparative International Development, Spring 1973, pp. 71-87.

Frías, Ismael. La revolución peruana y la vía socialista. Lima: Editorial Horizonte, 1970.

García, José Z. "Military Government in Peru, 1968-1971." Unpublished doctoral dissertation, University of New Mexico, 1973.

Graham Hurtado, José. Filosofía de la revolución peruana. Lima: Oficina Nacional de Información, 1971.

Handleman, Howard. Struggle in the Andes: Peasant Political Mobilization in Peru. Austin: University of Texas Institute of Latin American Studies, Monograph 35, 1975.

Matos Mar, José. Perú problema no. 1: 5 ensayos. Lima: Instituto de Estudios Peruanos, 1968.

Quijano Obregón, Aníbal. "Contemporary Peasant Movements," in Seymour Martin Lipset and Aldo Solari, eds., Elites in Latin America. New York: Oxford University Press, 1967.

Taylor, Milton. "Problems of Development in Peru," Journal of Inter-American Studies, January 1967, pp. 85-94.

Thorp, Rosemary. "A Note on Food Supplies, the Distribution of Income, and National Income Accounting in Peru," Bulletin of the Oxford University Institute of Economics and Statistics, November 1969, pp. 229-241.

Bibliography   142

Van de Wetering, Hylke. "Agricultural Planning: the Peru-
    vian Experience," in Eric Thorbecke, ed., The Role of
    Agriculture in Economic Development. National Bureau
    for Economic Research, 1969.

4. Mass Media and Public Opinion

Alisky, Marvin. "Broadcasting in Peru," Journal of Broad-
    casting, Spring 1959, pp. 118-127.

_____. "Government-Press Relations in Peru," Journalism
    Quarterly, Winter 1976, pp. 661-665.

_____. "The Mass Media," in Alisky, Peruvian Political
    Perspective, 2nd ed. Tempe: Arizona State University
    Center for Latin American Studies, 1975, pp. 25-28,
    35-36.

_____. "The Peruvian Press and the Nixon Incident,"
    Journalism Quarterly, Fall 1958, pp. 411-419.

Carty, Winthrop P. "Latin American Press Freedom Under
    Attack," Times of the Americas, December 10, 1975,
    p. 3.

Dickerson, Mark O. "Peru Institutes Social Property as Part
    of its 'Revolutionary Transformation,'" Inter-American
    Economic Affairs, Fall 1975, pp. 23-33.

Klarén, Peter F. Modernization, Dislocation, and Aprismo:
    Origins of the Peruvian Aprista Party, 1870-1932. Aus-
    tin: University of Texas Institute of Latin American
    Studies, Monograph 32, 1973.

Miró Quesada Laos, Carlos. Historia del periodismo peruano.
    Lima: Editorial Comercio, 1957.

5. Special Reports

Alberti, Giorgio. Inter-Village Systems and Development: a
    Study of Social Change in Highland Peru. Ithaca, N.Y.:
    Cornell University Latin American Studies Dissertation
    Series, 1970.

Austin, Allan G., and Lewis, Sherman. Urban Government

for Metropolitan Lima. New York: Praeger, 1970.

Bergman, Arlene, and Larson, Magali. Social Stratification in Peru. Berkeley: University of California Institute of International Studies, 1969.

Dickerson, Mark O. "Peru's Experiment in 'Revolution': the Quest for a Model." Unpublished paper at the meeting of the Canadian Political Science Association, Fredericton, New Brunswick, June 11, 1977.

Fitzgerald, E. V. K. The State and Economic Development: Peru Since 1968. London: Cambridge University Press, 1976.

Hayn, Rolf. "Peruvian Exchange Controls," Inter-American Economic Affairs, Spring 1957, pp. 47-70.

Knight, Peter T. "New Forms of Economic Organization in Peru: Toward Workers' Self-Management," in Abraham F. Lowenthal, ed., The Peruvian Experiment: Continuity and Change under Military Rule. Princeton, N. J.: Princeton University Press, 1975.

MacLean, Roberto G. Sociología del Perú. México, D. F.: Universidad Nacional Autónoma de México, 1959.

Malpica, Carlos. Los dueños del Perú, 3rd ed. Lima: Editorial Ensayos Sociales, 1968.

Niedergang, Marcel. "Revolutionary Nationalism in Peru," Foreign Affairs, April 1971, pp. 454-463.

North, Liisa. Civil-Military Relations in Argentina, Chile, and Peru. Berkeley: University of California Political of Modernization Series No. 2, 1966.

_____. "The Origins and Development of the Peruvian Aprista Party." Doctoral Dissertation, unpublished, University of California, Berkeley, 1973.

Orlove, Benjamin S. Alpacas, Sheep, and Men: Wool Export Economy and Regional Society in Southern Peru. New York: Academic Press, 1977.

Palmer, David Scott. "Peru: Authoritarianism and Reform," in Howard J. Wiarda and Harvey F. Kline, eds., Latin

American Politics and Development.   Boston: Houghton Mifflin, 1978.

_____. Revolution from Above: Military Government and Popular Participation in Peru, 1968-1972.   Ithaca, N. Y. : Cornell University Latin American Studies Dissertation Series, 1971.

_____, and Middlebrook, Kevin J.   Military Government and Political Development: Lessons from Peru.   Beverly Hills, Cal. : Sage Publications Comparative Politics Series, 1975.

_____, and Rodríguez, Jorge.   "The Peruvian Military Government: the Problems of Popular Participation," Bulletin of the Institute of Development Studies (University of Sussex), September 1972, pp. 4-15.

Pike, Frederick B.   "Peru and the Quest for Reform by Compromise," Inter-American Economic Affairs, Spring 1967.

Quijano Obregón, Aníbal.   Nacionalismo, neoimperialismo, y militarismo en el Perú.   Buenos Aires: Ediciones Periferia, 1971.

Van de Wetering, Hylke.   "The Current State of Land Reform in Peru," LTC Newsletter, April-June 1973, pp. 5-9.

Velasco Alvarado, Juan.   Velasco: la voz de la revolución. Lima: Editorial Ausonia, 1972.

6.   Legal Literature

Clagett, Helen L.   A Guide to the Law and Legal Literature of Peru.   Washington, D. C. : Library of Congress, 1947.

Eder, Phanor J.   A Comparative Survey of Anglo-American and Latin-American Law.   New York: New York University Press, 1950.

Leguía, Germán.   Nuevo diccionario de la legislación peruana. Lima: Editorial Lucero, 1921.

Valderrama, David M.   Law and Legal Literature of Peru:

a Revised Guide. Washington, D. C. : Library of Congress, 1976.

7. Reform Analysis

Aguirre Gamio, Hernando. "El proceso de la reforma agraria en el Perú," Mundo Nuevo, January 1970, pp. 24-35.

Ballantyne, Janet. "The Political Economy of Peruvian Gran Minería." Doctoral dissertation, unpublished, Cornell University School of Business, 1974.

Carpio Becerra, Alfredo. "La reform educativa en marcha," Ministerio de Educación Pública, March 1973.

Mesa-Lago, Carmelo. "Social Security Stratification and Inequality in Latin America: the Case of Peru." Mimeographed report, University of Pittsburgh Latin American Studies, 1973.

Stepan, Alfred. The State and Society: Peru in Comparative Perspective. Princeton, N. J. : Princeton University Press, 1978.

8. Foreign Relations

Carey, James C. Peru and the United States: 1900-1962. Notre Dame, Ind. : University of Notre Dame Press, 1964.

Dye, Richard W. "Peru, the United States, and Hemispheric Relations," Inter-American Economic Affairs, Autumn 1972, pp. 69-88.

Needler, Martin. "U. S. Recognition Policy and the Peruvian Case," Inter-American Economic Affairs, April 1963.

Patch, Richard. "The Peruvian Earthquake of 1970," American Universities Field Staff Newsletter, Vol. 18, Parts 1-4, March to July 1971, Nos. 6-9.

Pike, Frederick B. The United States and the Andean Republics. Cambridge: Harvard University Press, 1977.

Sharp, Daniel A. , ed. U. S. Foreign Policy and Peru. Austin: University of Texas Press, 1972.

U. S. Congress, Senate Committee on Foreign Relations.
       United States Relations with Peru. Hearings Before the
       Subcommittee on Western Hemisphere Affairs, 91st Con-
       gress, 1st Session, Washington, D. C. , April 14-17,
       1969.

9. History

a) Colonial

Albenino, Nicholás de. Verdadera relación de lo sussedido
       en los reynos e provincias del Perú. Sevilla: original
       edition, 1549. English facsimile edition printed in Bos-
       ton, 1930.

Arriaga, Pablo José de. Extirpación de la idolatría del Perú.
       Lima: Society of Jesus, 1621.

Bennett, Wendell. Ancient Arts of the Andes. New York:
       Museum of Modern Art, 1954.

Bird, Junius, and Bennett, Wendell C. Andean Cultural His-
       tory. New York: Museum of Natural History Handbook
       Series, No. 15, 1949.

Calancha, Antonio de la. Crónica moralizada del orden de
       San Augustín en el Perú, con sucesos ejemplares. Bar-
       celona: Augustinian Order in Spain, 1638.

Campbell, Leon G. The Military and Society in Colonial
       Peru, 1750-1810. Philadelphia: American Philosophical
       Society Memoirs, 1978.

Cieza de León, Pedro. La crónica del Perú. Sevilla: Part
       I, 1553. Edition printed in London in 1709.

_____. Travels of Pedro de Cieza de León. Translated
       by Clements R. Markham. London: Hakluyt Society,
       1864. Newer translation by Harriet de Onis and edited
       by Victor Wolfgang von Hagen, Norman, Oklahoma:
       University of Oklahoma Press, 1957.

Fernández, Diego. Primera y segunda parte de la historia
       del Perú. Sevilla: 2 vols. , 1571.

García, Gregorio de. Origen de los indios. Valencia: Juan de Betanzos Manuscript, 1607.

Garcilaso de la Vega. Comentarios reales de los Incas. Lisbon: Part I, 1609.

_____. Historia general del Perú. Córdoba: Part II of Comentarios, 1617.

_____. Royal Commentaries of the Incas. Austin: University of Texas Press, 1953.

Gutiérrez de Santa Clara, Pedro. Historia de las guerras civiles del Perú y de otros sucesos de las indias. Madrid: 6 vols. , 1904-1929.

Means, Philip Ainsworth. An Account of the Conquest of Peru. New York: Cortés Society, 1917.

_____. Ancient Civilizations of the Andes. New York: Charles Scribner's Sons, 1931.

Meléndez, Juan de. Tesoros verdaderos de las indias en la historia de la gran provincia de San Juan Bautista del Perú. Rome: 3 vols. , 1681 and 1682.

Montesinos, Fernando. Los anales del Perú. Madrid: 2 vols. , 1906.

_____. Memorias antiguas historiales y políticas del Perú. Buenos Aires: Society of Jesus, 1870.

Palma, Ricardo. Anales de la inquisición de Lima. Lima, 1863.

_____. Perú. Madrid: 6 vols. , 1923.

_____. Perú: Tradiciones. Lima: 2 vols. , 1875 and 1877. Second edition, 1883.

Paz Soldán, Marino Felipe. Historia del Perú independiente, 1822-1827. Lima: 3 vols. , 1868-1874. Reprinted, Lima: 2 vols. , 1919. New edition, Lima: 3 vols. , 1929.

Peralta Barnuevo Rocha, Pedro. Lima fundada. Lima: 2 vols. , 1723.

Bibliography 148

Pizarro, Pedro. Relación del descubrimiento y conquista del Perú. English edition edited by Philip A. Means, New York: 2 vols., 1921.

Poma de Ayala, Felipe Huamán. Nueva crónica y buen gobierno. Paris: Pietschmann Manuscript, 1936.

Prado y Ugarteche, Javier. Estado social del Perú durante la dominación española. Lima: Prado, 1894.

Prescott, William H. History of the Conquest of Peru. New York: Random House, Modern Library Edition, 1936.

Riva Agüero, José de la. (Under pen name P. Pruvonena.) Memorias y documentos para la historia de la independencia del Perú. Paris: 2 vols., 1858.

Sarmiento de Gamboa, Pedro. Segunda parte de la historia general llamada índica. Berlin: Geschichte, 1906.

Toribio Medina, José. Colección de historiadores de Chile. Santiago: Volume 27, Peru, 1901.

Torres, Bernardo de. Crónica de la provincia peruana del orden de los ermitaños de San Augustín. Lima: Augustinian Order, 1657.

Unánue, José Hipólito. Guia política, eclesiástica y militar del Perú. Lima: 5 vols., 1793-1797.

Von Hagen, Victor W. Highway of the Sun. New York: Duell, Sloan, and Pearce, 1955.

_____. Realm of the Incas. New York: Mentor New American Library, 1957.

Wilgus, A. Curtis. Histories and Historians of Hispanic America. New York: H. W. Wilson Publishing Company, 1942. Sections on 16th, 17th, and 18th Century historians.

_____. The Historiography of Latin America. A Guide to Historical Writing, 1500-1800. Metuchen, N.J.: Scarecrow Press, 1975.

Zárate, Augustín de. Historia del descubrimiento y conquista de la provincia del Perú. Antwerp, 1555. Spanish edi-

tions, Sevilla 1577 and Madrid 1853. An English translation is in Robert Kerr, A General History and Collection of Voyages, Edinburgh, 1824.

b) Since Independence

Alba, Víctor. Peru. Boulder, Col. : Westview Press, 1977.

Alianza Acción Popular-Demócrata Cristiano. Bases para el
Plan de Gobierno.

Barreda Laos, Felipe. Vida intelectual del virreinato del
Perú. Buenos Aires, 1937.

Basadre, Jorge. Historia de la república del Perú. Lima:
Editorial Universitaria, 1964-1970, 19 vols.

_____. Historia del derecho peruano. Lima: Editorial
Antería, 1937. 2-vol. edition of the Biblioteca Peruana
de Ciencias Jurídicas y Sociales, 1937.

_____. La iniciación de la república. Lima: 2 vols.,
1928 and 1929.

_____. La multitud, la ciudad y el campo en la historia
del Perú. Lima, 1929.

_____. Perú: problema y posibilidad. Lima, 1931.

Basadre, Modesto. Diez años de historia política del Perú,
1834-44. Lima: Revised Edition, 1953.

Bejar Rivera, Héctor. Perú 1965. México, D. F. : Siglo
Veintiuno, 1969.

Belaúnde, Fernando. Peru's Own Conquest. Lima:
American Studies Press, 1965.

Belaúnde, Víctor Andrés. Mi generación en la universidad.
Lima, 1961.

_____. La realidad nacional. Lima: Mercurio,
1930.

Bulnes, Gonzalo. Bolívar en el Perú. Madrid, 1897.

Bustamante y Rivero, José Luis. Tres años de lucha por la democracia en el Perú. Buenos Aires. 1949.

Cappa, Ricardo. Historia del Perú. Lima, 1886.

Casós, Fernando. La revolución de julio en el Perú. Valparaíso: Empresa de Chile, 1872.

Chirinos Soto, Enrique. Cuenta y balance de las elecciones de 1962. Lima: Ediciones Perú, 1962.

_____. El Perú frente a junio de 1962. Lima: Tribuna, 1962.

Comité de Asesoramiento de la Presidencia de la República. La revolución nacional peruana: 1968-1972. Lima: COAP, 1972.

Cornejo Chávez, Héctor. Qué se propone la Democracia Cristiana. Lima: Ediciones del Sol, 1962.

Dávilos y Lissón, Pedro. Historia republicana del Perú. Lima: 10 vols., 1931 to 1939.

_____. Primera centuria; material del Perú en el primer siglo de su independiencia. Lima: 8 vols., 1919 to 1938.

Davis, Harold E., Finan, J.J., and Peck, F. T., eds. Latin American Diplomatic History. Baton Rouge: Louisiana State University Press, 1977.

Delgado, Luis Humberto. Historia de los gobiernos del Perú y de las presidentes de las cámaras legislativas, 1921-1927. Lima: 2 vols., 1927, 1928.

_____. Historia republicana del Perú, 1821-1933. Lima, 1933.

Fermandoiz, José Luis. El conflicto eclesiástico de Tacna. Santiago: Tacna-Arica, 1923.

García Calderón, Francisco. Le Perou Contemporain. Paris: Ecrivain, 1907.

González Prada, Manuel. Anarquía. Lima: Published Posthumously, 1936.

151   Bibliography

_____. Horas de lucha. Lima, 1908.

_____. Páginas libres. Lima, 1894.

_____. Propaganda y ataque. Lima: Published Posthumously, 1938.

Haya de la Torre, Víctor Raúl. Construyendo el aprismo: artículos y cartas desde el exilio, 1924-31. Buenos Aires, 1933.

_____. Ideología aprista. Lima, 1961.

_____. Pensamiento político de Haya de la Torre. Lima: APRA, 5 vols., 1961.

_____. Teoría y táctica del aprismo. Lima: Editorial Cahuide, 1931.

Herbold, Carl, Jr., and Stein, Steven. Guía bibliográfica para la historia social y política del Perú en el siglo XX. Lima: Ediciones Campodónico for the Instituto de Estudios Peruanos, 1971.

Houtart, Francisco. El cambio social en América Latina. Bogotá: Estudios Socio-Religiosos Latino Americanos, No. 18, 1964.

Inman, Samuel Guy. South America Today. New York: Committee on Cooperation in Latin America, 1921.

Juan, Jorge, and Ulloa, Antonio de. A Voyage to South America. 5th ed. London: 2 vols., 1807.

Karno, Howard. "Augusto B. Leguía: the Oligarchy and the Modernization of Peru, 1870-1930." Doctoral dissertation, unpublished, University of California at Los Angeles, 1970.

Klaiber, Jeffrey L. Religion and Revolution in Peru, 1824-1976. Notre Dame, Indiana: University of Notre Dame Press, 1977.

Labarthe, Manuel. Pedro Gálvez y la abolición del tributo indígena. Lima: Ediciones del Sol, 1954.

Leguía, Jorge Guillermo. Estudios históricos. Lima: Leguía, 1939.

La Prensa. Lima daily newspaper La Prensa for November 9, 1945: collection of essays on education of the 1890s by Víctor A. Belaúnde, José Gálvez, Jorge Basadre, and Raúl Porras.

Lohmann Villena, Guillermo. El corregidor de indios en el Perú bajo los austrias. Madrid, 1957.

Lorente, Sebatián. Historia del Perú bajo los Borbones. Lima, 1871.

Mariátegui, José Carlos. Siete ensayos de interpretación de la realidad peruana. 2nd ed. Lima: Editorial Librería Peruana, 1934.

Martín, José Carlos. José Pardo y Barreda. Lima: Biografía, 1948.

Martin, Percy F. Peru in the Twentieth Century. London, 1911.

Mecham, J. Lloyd. Church and State in Latin America. 2nd ed. Chapel Hill, N.C.: University of North Carolina Press, 1966.

Miró Quesada Laos, Carlos. Autopsía de los partidos políticos. Lima: Editorial Comercio, 1961.

Miró Quesada Sosa, Aurelio. Costa, sierra, y montaña. Lima: Editorial Comercio, 1947.

Moore, John P. The Cabildo in Peru. Durham, N.C.: Duke University Press, 1954.

Neira, Hugo. Cuzco: tierra y muerte. Lima: Populibros Peruanos, 1964.

Odriozola, Manuel de, ed. Documentos históricos del Perú en las épocas del coloniaje ... y de la independencia hasta la presente. Lima: 10 vols. , 1863-1877.

Owens, R. J. Peru. London: Oxford University Press, 1963.

Palma, Ricardo. Anales de la inquisición de Lima. Lima, 1863.

153   Bibliography

Palma, Ricardo. Perú: tradiciones. Lima: 2 vols., 1875 and 1877. Second edition, Lima: 6 vols., 1883. Third edition, Madrid: 6 vols., 1923.

_____. Refutación a un compendio de historia del Perú. Lima, 1869.

Pareja Paz Soldán, José. Las constituciones del Perú. Madrid, 1954.

_____, ed. Visión del Perú en el siglo XX. Lima: 2 vols., 1962.

Payne, Arnold. The Peruvian Coup d'Etat of 1962. Washington, D. C.: Institute for the Comparative Study of Political Systems, 1968.

Paz Soldán, Marino Felipe. Historia del Perú independiente, 1822-1827. Lima: 3 vols., 1968-1974.

Pike, Frederick B. The Modern History of Peru. New York: Praeger, 1967.

_____. "The Modernized Church in Peru: Two Aspects," The Review of Politics, July 1964, pp. 307-318.

_____. "The Old and the New APRA in Peru," Inter-American Economic Affairs, August 1964.

_____. "Peru and the Quest for Reform by Compromise," Inter-American Economic Affairs, Spring 1967.

Porras Barrenechea, Raúl. Fuentes históricas peruanas. Lima: Revised Edition, 1963.

_____. Mito, tradición e historia del Perú. Lima, 1951.

Reyna, Alberto W. Historia diplomática del Perú. Lima: 2 vols., 1964.

Riva Agüero, José de la. La Historia en el Perú. Lima: Universidad Mayor de San Marcos, 1910. Reprinted in 1952.

_____. Memorias y documentos para la historia de la independencia del Perú. Paris: 2 vols., 1847, and New York: 2 vols., 1847.

Bibliography   154

Romero, Emilio. Geografía económica del Perú. Lima:
Revised Edition, 1961.

_____. Historia económica del Perú. Lima, 1949.

Sánchez, Luis Alberto. Breve noticia de la fundación y trans-
formaciones de la facultad de filosofía y letras. Lima:
Universidad Nacional Mayor de San Marcos Filosofía y
Letras, 1918.

_____. Haya de la Torre y el apra. Santiago: Biblio-
teca América, 1934. Revised edition, 1955.

_____. Perú, retrato de un país adolescente. Lima, 1963.

Stanger, F. M. "Church and State in Peru," Hispanic American Historical Review, November 1927.

Steward, Julian H., ed. The Andean Civilization. Washington, D. C. : Smithsonian Institution, 1946.

Stuart, Graham H. The Governmental System of Peru.
Washington, D. C. : Carnegie Institution of Washington,
1925.

Sulmont, Denis. El movimiento obrero en el Perú, 1900-
1956. Lima: Pontificia Universidad Católica del Perú,
1975.

Tibesar, Antanine. Franciscan Beginnings in Peru. Washington, D. C. : Franciscan History, 1953.

Tovar, Manuel. Apuntes para la historia eclesiástica del
Perú hasta el gobierno del VII arzobispo. Lima: 2
vols., 1873 and 1876.

Urteaga, Horacio. El imperio incaico. Lima, 1931.

Valega, José M. El virreinato del Perú. Lima, 1939.

Vargas, José M. La gesta emancipadora del Perú. Lima:
12 vols., 1940-1943.

Vargas U., Nemesio. Historia del Perú independiente.
Lima: 8 vols., 1903-1917.

Vargas, Ugarte, Rubén. Historia del Perú. Lima: Libros
de Texto, 1939.

155   Bibliography

Velasco, Juan de. La historia del reino de Quito en la
América meridional. Quito: 3 vols., 1841-1844.

Villanueva, Victor. El militarismo en el Perú. Lima: Empresa Gráfica Scheuch, 1962.

Werlich, David P. Peru: a Short History. Carbondale,
Ill.: Southern Illinois University Press, 1978.

Whitaker, Arthur P. The Huancavelica Mercury Mine. Cambridge: Harvard University Press, 1941.

Wiese, Carlos. Las civilizaciones primitivas del Perú.
Lima, 1913.

_____. Historia del Perú. Lima: 4 vols., 1925-1928.

_____. Historia del Perú independiente. Lima, 1925.

_____. Historia del Perú y de la civilización peruana.
Lima, 1917.

Wright, Marie. The Old and New Peru. Philadelphia, 1908.

Zimmerman, A. F. Francisco de Toledo. Caldwell, Idaho,
1938.

10. Bibliographies

Basadre, Jorge. "Notas sobre la experiencia histórica peruana," Revista Histórica (Lima), Vol. XIX, 1952,
pp. 5-140.

Biblioteca Central de la Universidad Nacional Mayor de San
Marcos. Boletín Bibliográfico. Periodical, 1923-1968,
1972-.

Biblioteca Nacional de Lima. Anuario Bibliografíco Peruano.
Lima: Biblioteca Nacional, 1957-.

_____. Boletín Bibliográfico. Periodical, irregular inter-
vals, 1919-1920, 1943-.

Pacheco Vélez, César. "La historiografía peruana contem-
poranea," in José Pareja Paz Soldán, ed., Visión del
Perú en el siglo XX. Lima: Vol. 2, 1962.

Paz Soldán, Mariano Felipe. Biblioteca peruana. Lima,
    1879.

Sainte Marie S. , Dario, ed. Perú en cífras. Lima, 1945.

Tauro, Alberto. Bibliografía peruana de historia, 1940-53.
    Lima, 1954.

_____. Historia e historiadores del Perú. Lima, 1957.

11. Current Sources on Peru

a) Peruvian

Caretas. Published twice a month in Lima. Published at
    Camana 615, Oficina 308.

The Lima Times. (Formerly the Peruvian Times and Andean
    Air Mail). Published weekly in Lima at Carabaya 928,
    Third Floor.

b) U. S.

Diario de las Américas. A daily Spanish-language newspaper
    published in Miami, Florida, with news of Peru found
    on page 2 almost daily.

Facts on File. An indexed weekly digest of news. Found in
    every university library and most other U. S. libraries.

Latin American Digest. Published four times a year by the
    Arizona State University Center for Latin American
    Studies, Tempe, Arizona.

Miami Herald. The only daily newspaper in the United States
    to publish a page of news about Latin America every
    day of the year. Peruvian news appears frequently.
    Published in Miami, Florida.

Times of the Americas. Published twice a month in Wash-
    ington, D. C. at the Woodward Building. It runs nothing
    but news in English of Latin America gleaned from United
    Press International, Associated Press, Reuters, Copley
    News Service, and its own correspondents.

157   Bibliography

c) British

Latin America Economic Report.   Published weekly by Latin
American Newsletters Ltd. in London.   U. S. subscrip-
tions: 432 Park Avenue South, New York, N. Y. 10016.

Latin America Political Report.   Published weekly by Latin
American Newsletters Ltd. in London.   U. S. subscrip-
tions: 432 Park Avenue South, New York, N. Y. 10016.